www.getmapping.com

Racecourses

by John White

AINTREE
ASCOT
AYR
BANGOR-ON-DEE
BATH
BEVERLEY
BRIGHTON
CARLISLE
CARTMEL
CATTERICK BRIDGE
CHELTENHAM
CHEPSTOW
CHESTER
CURRAGH, THE
DONCASTER
EPSOM DOWNS
EXETER
FAKENHAM
FOLKESTONE
FONTWELL PARK
GALWAY
GOODWOOD
HAMILTON PARK
HAYDOCK PARK
HEREFORD
HEXHAM
HUNTINGDON
KELSO
KEMPTON PARK
LEICESTER
LEOPARDSTOWN
LIMERICK
LINGFIELD PARK
LISTOWEL
LUDLOW
MARKET RASEN
MUSSELBURGH
NAAS
NEWBURY
NEWCASTLE
NEWMARKET

NEWTON ABBOT
NOTTINGHAM
PERTH
PLUMPTON
PONTEFRACT
PUNCHESTOWN
REDCAR
RIPON
SALISBURY
SANDOWN PARK
SEDGEFIELD
SOUTHWELL
STRATFORD-ON-AVON
TAUNTON
THIRSK
TOWCESTER
TRALEE
UTTOXETER
WARWICK
WETHERBY
WINCANTON
WINDSOR
WOLVERHAMPTON
WORCESTER
YARMOUTH
YORK

www.getmapping.com

Racecourses

by John White

First published in 2003 by
HarperCollins Publishers
77-85 Fulham Palace Road
London W6 8JB

The Collins website is
www.collins.co.uk

Collins is a registered trademark of HarperCollins Publishers.

Photography © 2003 Getmapping plc
Cartography © 2003 HarperCollins Publishers Ltd

Getmapping plc hereby asserts its moral right to be identified as the author of this work.

Text © 2003 John White
John White hereby asserts his moral right to be identified as the author of this work.

Irish aerial photography
Galway, Leopardstown, Limerick, Listowel, Naas, Tralee
© BKS Survey Ltd. **www.bks.co.uk**
The Curragh © jasonhawkes.com
Punchestown © Peter Barrow

Getmapping can produce an individual print of any area shown in this book, or of any area within the United Kingdom. The image can be centred wherever you choose, printed at any size from A6 to 7.5 metres square, and at any scale up to 1:1,000. For further information, please contact Getmapping on 01530 835685 or log on to **www.getmapping.com**.

A CIP catalogue record for this book is available from the British Library.

ISBN 0 00 716655 9

Design by Colin Brown
Colour origination by Colourscan, Singapore
Printed and bound, by Editoriale Johnson, Italy

**For my Uncle Jeff
and Aunt Frances**

I am grateful to Tom Whiting, Céire Clark and Philip Parker, my Managing Editor – all at HarperCollins Publishers. I have also received some generous assistance and kind help with Irish racecourses from Nessie Bergin of 'The Irish Field'. Geoff Johnson of Weatherbys has again done much to help me.

John White

Contents

Course locator map

Perth

Musselburgh

Hamilton Park

Kelso

Ayr

Hexham Newcastle

Carlisle

Sedgefield Redcar

Catterick Bridge

Cartmel Thirsk

Ripon

Wetherby York

Beverley

Pontefract

Galway Aintree Doncaster Market Rasen

Leopardstown Haydock Park

Chester Southwell

Naas Bangor-on-Dee Uttoxeter Nottingham

The Curragh Punchestown Leicester Fakenham

Wolverhampton Huntingdon

Limerick Yarmouth

Listowel Ludlow Warwick

Tralee Worcester Newmarket

Hereford Towcester

Stratford-on-Avon

Cheltenham

Chepstow Windsor Kempton Park

Newbury Sandown Park

Bath Ascot Lingfield Park

Salisbury Epsom Downs Folkestone

Taunton Plumpton

Wincanton Goodwood Brighton

Fontwell Park

Exeter

Newton Abbot

Foreword

With their often ancient origins, innovatory nature and rich reflections of the culture, history, way of life and sporting preferences of those attending them, British and Irish Racecourses are, quite simply, the best in the world. Their often scenic settings, topographical variety and impressive vistas make the more than 60 racecourses featured in this book a wonder to behold. This is because for the very first time detailed course maps for use 'on the ground' are combined with full colour aerial views and a descriptive text designed to do full justice to the nature, idiosyncrasies, history, charms and major attractions of the many places in Britain and Ireland where the thrill of seeing racehorses in action can be experienced.

The fact that Airborne won the first post-war Derby with all four feet in the air and that Aintree was used for flying displays before the First World War provide just two examples of the close link between racecourses and the airspaces over them. Landings by fixed-wing aircraft and by helicopters on designated areas of racetracks are now a routine part of the thrilling experience that going to the races provides. On big race days hot air balloons provide the type of 'bird's-eye' views with which this book is packed. In a chapter of his autobiography entitled 'Crash Landing', jockey, Barry Brogan recalls his desperate dash from Perth, where he had won the 5.15, to distant Wolverhampton to take a mount in the 7.45. At 7.10 Brogan was still in the air but persuaded his pilot to make an 'emergency' landing on an on-course soccer pitch! Ironically, Brogan was sent flying in the race and was fined £150 for his rule-breaking. For a fraction of that sum, readers of this book can look down on the racecourses of Britain and Ireland and, without feeling a moment's anxiety, really savour the experience.

John White, June 2003

Aintree

Aintree Racecourse
Ormskirk Road
Aintree
Liverpool L9 5AS
Tel: (0151) 523 2600
www.aintree.co.uk

HOW TO GET THERE:
From North: M6 (Junct. 26); M58
From South: M6 (Junct. 21A); M62
(Junct. 6); M57 (Junct. 7)
From East: M62 (Junct. 6); M57
(Junct. 7)
From West: A5036
By Rail: Aintree (via Liverpool
Central)
By Air: Liverpool John Lennon
Airport; Helicopter facilities on
course – telephone the race-
course on the above number

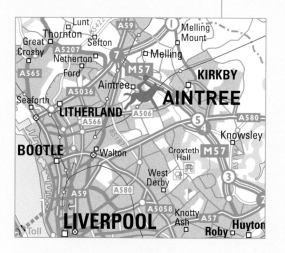

As the home of the Grand National, the world's most famous and widely watched horserace staged on Merseyside as one of the rites of spring, Aintree (originally 'one tree') is a suitably singular racecourse that is formidably reflective of its Viking ancestry. As enigmatic and paradoxical as it is unparalleled, this is a course that offers its visitors even more surprises, delights and occasional disappointments than vastly dissimilar Epsom where the Derby is staged just two months after the National.

Still accessible by rail (as it was when the first 'Grand Liverpool' steeplechase there was one by the appropriately named Lottery in 1839), the course can no longer be reached by paddleboat via a nearby canal. Instead, the vast majority of the thousands of modern-day racegoers who flock to the again-flourishing three-day Spring Festival arrive by car. Perhaps mindful of the fact that Aintree was used for flying displays as early as 1909, a minority of racegoers (among them that small number of National Hunt jockeys who are sufficiently affluent to do so) arrive at the course by air, disembarking from helicopters that land on part of a six-acre enclosure. Small fixed-wing aircraft can land seven miles from Speke, while arrivals at Manchester airport can avoid a 40-mile road journey by making prior arrangements. One of the biggest surprises to Aintree's first-time visitor is that there are, in fact, three courses, all left-handed but otherwise very dissimilar. The Grand National is run over 4½ miles – the longest race distance to be found in Britain. It involves the separate National course whose distinctive, formidable and famous fences (among them the Chair, Valentine's and Becher's Brook) are not negotiated by the steeplechasers that run on the separate Mildmay course (named after perhaps the unluckiest jockey not to have won the National). This course, a 1½ mile fairly rectangular affair that features sharper turns and rather less taxing fences of the type found on many park courses elsewhere, tends to favour fast, front-running chasers since these are seldom overhauled on the final, short 260-yard run-in.

It is, of course, a far different story over the National course, as was spectacularly demonstrated in 1973 when perhaps the unluckiest equine loser of Aintree's big race – the gallant runaway top-weight Crisp – was finally caught at the death by Red Rum who prevailed in a then record-winning time.

Like many a tiring National leader before him, Crisp found the gruelling long 494-yard Aintree run-in all against him. Indeed, this particularly taxing final demand on a horse's stamina and courage does much still to ensure that, even though radical alterations were made to many fences featured in the National prior to its 1990 run-in, this race will present steeplechasers with an extremely searching test.

Aintree's hurdle course – a far from tight affair that extends for approximately 10 furlongs – is as flat as both the Mildmay and National steeplechasing courses and, like the latter, features a testingly long run-in.

Aintree's topography, it must be said, tends to interfere with the view of many of its patrons, which is one reason why giant television screens have been erected in some public enclosures. Indeed, those sufficiently fortunate, affluent and foresighted to find themselves in one of the many tents, boxes, chalets and hospitality suites beloved of Aintree's many corporate entertainers are far less likely to get an interrupted or indistinct view of the racing, but may well go for the less sophisticated and cheaper pleasure of picnicking point-to-point style close to a formidable fence and then watch the rest of the big race in thrilling close-up on a portable television.

The fact that bear-baiting and cock-fighting took place at Aintree perhaps explains why the sport that has superceded them there is enjoyed in such a hedonistic and informal manner. Other than the avoidance of nudity, as occasionally favoured by the odd drunken streaker, no restrictions are placed on the dress of racegoers. Children are admitted free at all meetings, save on Grand National day itself, and disabled racegoers are well catered for. Most appropriately, too, given the

AINTREE: Plan of the course, which includes the Grand National course.

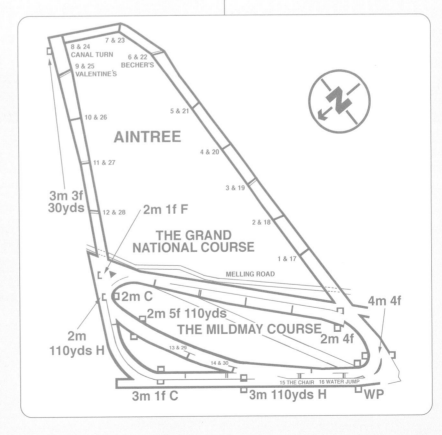

National's recent 150th running, Aintree also has its own racing museum.

From 1972 until 1992, the Spring Festival was the only meeting staged at Liverpool all season. Justly billed as offering 'three days of top-class competitive racing', its thrilling last-day finale is, of course, the National. However, on each of the two days prior to this, a taste of the real thing to follow is provided by a race run over some of the National's fences. Becher's, Valentine's and the Chair are all jumped during the John Hughes Memorial Chase (formerly the Topham Chase) on the Thursday and also on the following day in the amateurs' Grand National, the Foxhunter Chase.

Top-class pattern races for established stars and would-be ones and the inclusion of a championship event for horses that have run in National Hunt flat races do much to ensure that the two-day prelude to Grand National day is suitably exciting. As for the rest of the Saturday card, the Aintree Chase for top-class 2-mile 'chasers and the Aintree Hurdle for high-class 2½-mile hurdlers do much to make the meeting even more memorable.

The Chair is the course's widest obstacle.

Valentine's Brook. During the 1840 Grand National, on the approach to the second brook at Aintree, Valentine came to a sudden halt and yet managed to corkscrew over the obstacle. Hence another Aintree fence was christened.

Canal Turn

Becher's Brook. In the first Grand National (1839) Captain Becher on Conrad followed the race leader towards the first brook. Here Becher fell and crawled towards the deepest part of the brook to escape the hooves of his pursuers. He later said that never had water without whiskey tasted so foul. He managed to remount but got a second soaking when falling at the second brook.

Aintree

Aintree

Ascot

Ascot is located some 26 miles from London and affords access by road, rail and air (through its helicopter pad). It offers excellent facilities and viewing and provides arguably the best racing in Europe.

Races on this Group One, rather triangular-looking track of 1 mile 6 furlongs 34 yards are run either on the straight mile course or on sections of the round course. A spur provides the former section which is known as the Royal Hunt Cup course after a prestigious handicap staged at the Royal Meeting. This straight presents a stiff test to those running on it since they have to cope with some rising ground. The round course, which is used for races of 1, 1¼, 1½, 2 miles 45 yards, 2½ miles and 2 miles 6 furlongs 34 yards, is also undulating.

As can be readily appreciated, Ascot places a high premium on jockeyship. Horses running on the round course must be kept clear of converging rivals as they round the final bend and should not be asked to make up too much leeway in the mere 2½ furlongs that remain. On the straight course, the sheer width of the track means that horses tend to race in two distinct groups and an inexperienced jockey may, in moving his mount from one side of the track to another, inadvertently extend the distance over which it has to race by a quite alarming proportion.

To some extent Ascot represents a test of adaptability because of its short run-in, its undulations and its right-hand character. Above all, perhaps, it puts the stamina of horses on trial since it is essentially stiff, even severe, if the going is heavy. In general it tends to suit strong, resolute and long-striding gallopers rather than animals which appreciate tighter and less sweeping bends.

As for the draw, this is generally believed to confer no major advantage. However, if there is some give in the ground and the stalls are in a central position, low numbers may enjoy an advantage in the relatively short races that are staged on the straight course. Since Ascot is a right-hand track, it is also conceivable that high-drawn horses may be marginally favoured in longer races over the round course.

Some backers consider that the fiercely competitive nature of racing at Ascot and the fact that the right-handed course is so demanding conspire to cause rather too many upsets in form – a large number of which have come to be associated with many races, particularly big handicaps, that are staged at the Royal Meeting.

Ascot Racecourse
Ascot
Berkshire SL5 7JX
Tel: (01344) 622211, 876876
www.ascot.co.uk

HOW TO GET THERE:
From North: M1; M25 (Junct. 13)
From South: A3; M3 (Junct. 6)
From East: M3 (Junct. 3); A322; A332
From West: M4 (Junct. 6)
By Rail: Ascot (seven minutes' walk to racecourse)
By Air: Helicopter facilities

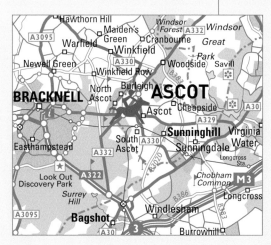

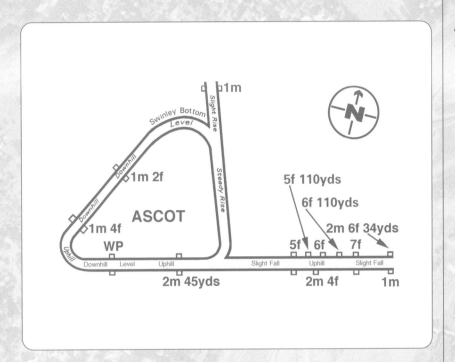

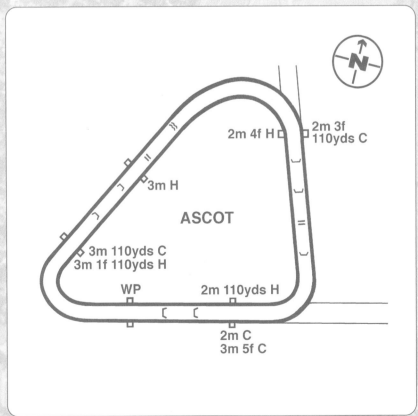

ASCOT: Plans of the Flat course (left) and the National Hunt course (below).

The luck of the Irish seems to hold good on the Berkshire course, where their runners often manage to improve by several pounds on their past running, so specially prepared are they to put up superlative performances. At few other racecourses in the world are so many valuable and prestigious races run in such a short space of time as is the case during the five-day Royal fixture that forms such a colourful and fashionable highlight of the social season.

Despite the formality that is de rigueur in the Royal Enclosure, the mid-June meeting is a far from stuffy affair. Although pomp and circumstance do put in an appearance at the Heath, they do so in the acceptably picturesque shape of the Windsor greys that on each day of the Royal Meeting pull the open landaus in which the Queen, the Duke of Edinburgh and other members of the Royal Family travel past the stands on their way to their private box.

Several famous stayers' races are staged during the June festival. By far the best known and the most prestigious is the Group One Ascot Gold Cup over 2½ miles which is run on ladies' day, traditionally the most fashionable of all. This race dates from 1807 and in its long history has produced thrillingly close finishes and even controversy, as was the case when Rock Roi was disqualified after winning on two separate occasions in 1971 and 1972.

In modern times no longer do Classic winners remain in training for a third season with the express aim of capturing this famous prize. However, that a Gold Cup was formerly regarded as furnishing conclusive proof of pre-eminence on the part of a thoroughbred is suggested by a glance at the record books. This will show that Persimmon (1897), Gay Crusader (1917), Gainsborough (1918), Owen Tudor (1942) and Ocean Swell (1945) all achieved the Derby Gold Cup double.

Since the vast majority of pattern races that attract the best modern British thoroughbreds involve contests of less than 2 miles – and sadly there has even been pressure to make this the maximum race distance – it may be unlikely that another Classic winner will ever add its name to this select group of staying champions.

After the Royal Meeting in June, the most prestigious is De Beers Diamond day in late July, the centrepiece of which is the Group One King George VI and Queen Elizabeth Diamond Stakes in which top-class thoroughbreds of three years and upwards from many parts of Europe compete over the Derby distance. Most appropriately, this race was won by Her Majesty the Queen's Aureole a year after the

coronation. So important is the King George VI and Queen Elizabeth Diamond Stakes that it is as highly regarded by top breeders in Kentucky's blue grass country as the Epsom Derby and Longchamp's Prix de l'Arc de Triomphe. Indeed, since its inception in 1951 the 'King George' has been won by no fewer than 14 Derby winners from Tulyar (1952) to Galileo 49 years later.

The so-called Festival of British Racing provides some top-class autumn racing for three days in late September. Some of its highlights are three races run over a mile – the Queen Elizabeth II Stakes, the Fillies' Mile and the Royal Lodge Stakes. The Diadem Stakes is a prestigious sprint, and yet another Festival race of note is the Cumberland Lodge Stakes of 12 furlongs.

Ascot is also a top-flight jumping course and on it are staged steeplechases that find out some inexperienced novices and present a true test of stamina on 'galloping' terrain. One such event, the Reynoldstown Novices 'chase, run in mid-February, recalls the dual (1935 and 1936) Grand National winner.

At no other racecourse in the world are so many historic, valuable and prestigious races run in such a short space of time as is the case during the four-day royal fixture that forms such a colourful and fashionable highlight of the social season.

Ascot

Ascot

Ayr

Ayr Racecourse
Western House
Whitletts Road
Ayr
KA8 0JE
Tel: (01292) 264179
www.ayr-racecourse.co.uk

HOW TO GET THERE:
From North: A78 (from
Greenock); A77 (from Glasgow)
From South: M6; M74 (Junct. 12);
A70
From East: A70
By Rail: Ayr
By Air: Glasgow Airport;
Helicopter facilities

Scotland's premier track, some 417 miles from London, can be reached by rail from Euston via Ayr station. It lies north-east of the town close to the A70 and A77. The course is an hour's drive from Glasgow and its landing strip can accommodate helicopters. It is a wide left-hand oval of 1 mile 4½ furlongs. The only undulations it features are rather gentle – indeed, its generally flat nature makes it a very fair track. Upsets in form cannot therefore justifiably be blamed on its conformation. Above all, the course is admirably suited to strong galloping types since its long run-in of around 4 furlongs gives a jockey sufficient time in which to make his or her run or the opportunity to ride a finely-judged waiting race. To the backer's advantage is the fact that the track dries out extremely quickly and thus the going is rarely heavy.

Various spurs provide straight stretches; on one that is especially wide 5 and 6 furlong events take place, while another gives opportunities to stage 10 and 11 furlong races which involve parts of the round course.

It is generally agreed that the draw does not greatly influence the results of races on this course. However, since places in the draw extend outwards from the left, low-drawn horses racing on the round sections on this left-handed course (over distances of 7 furlongs, 1 mile, 1 mile 5 furlongs 13 yards, 1 mile 7 furlongs and 2 miles 1 furlong 105 yards) may enjoy an understandable, if none too pronounced advantage. As for races over 5 and 6 furlongs on the straight course, the draw presents no appreciable advantage except perhaps when large fields face the starter. In such circumstances low numbers are preferable, especially if the stalls are positioned on the far side of the course and the going is soft.

Ayr does so much to stage attractive programmes that some trainers are fond of going north of the border and a few even nominate Ayr as their favourite racecourse.

The National Hunt highlight of Ayr's season is the Scottish Grand National which is often run in the sun of late April on going that is frequently firmer than that found at Aintree a few weeks earlier. Past winners often go in again in this 4 mile 1 furlong marathon.

The most prestigious race staged at Ayr on the flat is part of its three-day Western Meeting in late September. This, the Ayr Gold Cup, a 6-furlong cavalry charge of a sprint, first run in 1804, frequently falls to an improving three-year-old.

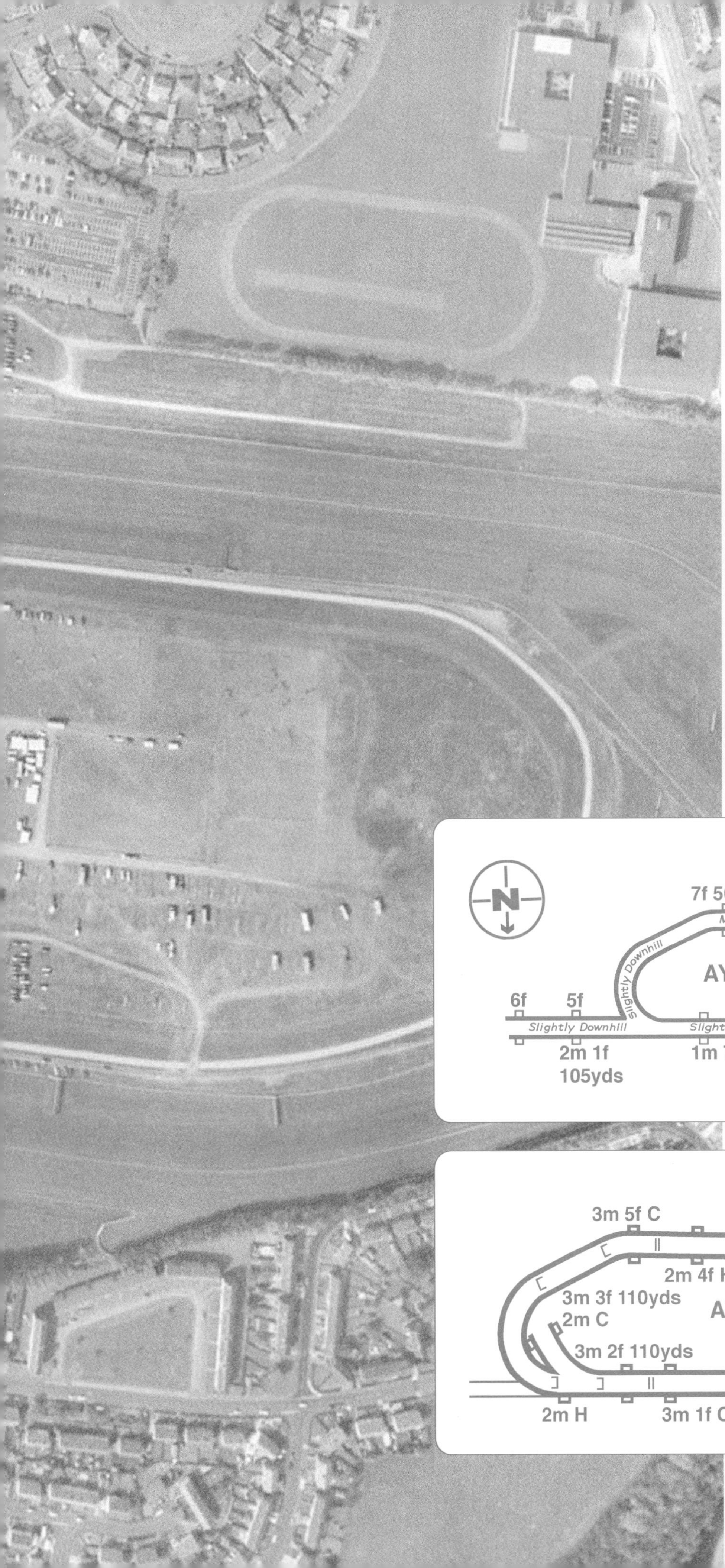

AYR: Plans of the Flat course (top), and the National Hunt course (bottom).

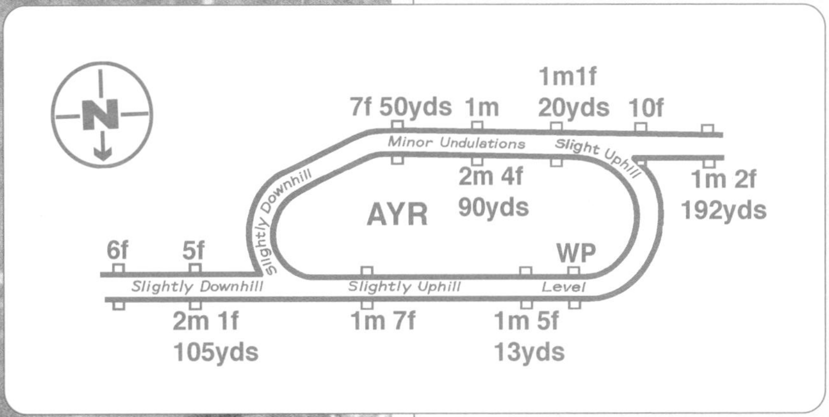

Flat course labels:
1m1f 20yds, 10f, 7f 50yds, 1m, Minor Undulations, Slight Uphill, 1m 2f 192yds, Slightly Downhill, 2m 4f 90yds, AYR, 6f, 5f, WP, Slightly Downhill, Slightly Uphill, Level, 2m 1f 105yds, 1m 7f, 1m 5f 13yds

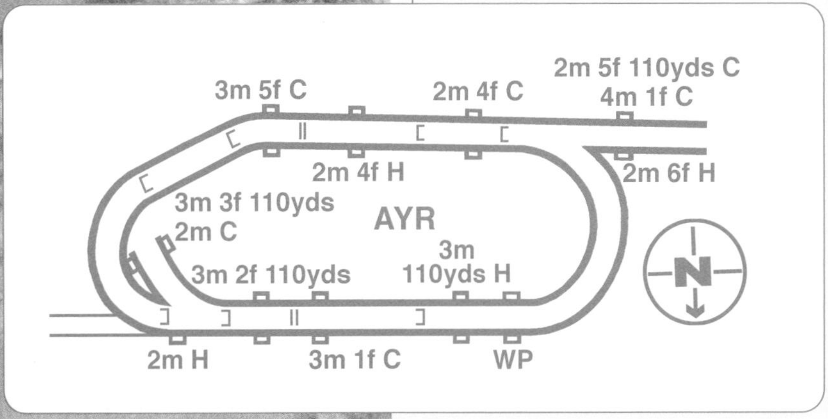

National Hunt course labels:
3m 5f C, 2m 4f C, 2m 5f 110yds C, 4m 1f C, 2m 4f H, 2m 6f H, 3m 3f 110yds, 2m C, AYR, 3m 110yds H, 3m 2f 110yds, 2m H, 3m 1f C, WP

[022] Ayr

Bangor-on-Dee

This track, where author Dick Francis had his first racecourse ride, is an unspoilt rustic gaff savoured by sporting racegoers who go there not to be seen but for the sake of meeting together and watching contests made the more sporting by their often fairly humble nature.

This Deeside course, which forms part of the pretty Bryn-y-Prys estate, is five miles from Wrexham. Bangor can be reached by rail via Wrexham station.

Those arriving by helicopter can land on course at Bangor where the absence of a grandstand is something of a downer when the heavens open, but it does mean that there is even more space for the delights of picnicking in point-to-point style on the side of one of the many old riverbanks that provide such an excellent view of the racing.

Straight sections of track are conspicuously absent at Bangor whose 1½-mile, mainly flat, track possesses a turn or two that approaches the tightness of the circuit at nearby Chester. The bends here are left-handed and the tightest is the Paddock bend.

As on many a sharpish track, front runners are often favoured here despite the fact that some can be finally pegged back on the longish 325-yard run-in. Its minor undulations and relatively easy fences – apart from an open ditch which finds out some suspect jumpers – means that this track is hardly a testing affair.

It is also most appropriate that, given its old-world charm, Sotheby & Co. have previously sponsored some races run on this beautiful racecourse. Such is their love of Bangor that some locals eschew the cover that cars provide in the wet. However, such spectators do so only from choice since Bangor now has a paddock restaurant and a new owners' and trainers' bar overlooking a new saddling ring. Bangor's increasing appeal means that leading trainers often run their promising novices on the course which stages the £20,000 Tote Handicap 'chase at a televised meeting in October.

Bangor-on-Dee Racecourse
Nr. Wrexham
N. Wales LL13 0DA
Tel: (01978) 780323
www.bangordee.co.uk

HOW TO GET THERE:
From North: M6 (Junct. 9); M56 (Junct. 15); M53; A483
From South: M6 (Junct. 15); A483 (from Wales)
From East: A525
From West: A5; A483; B5424
By Rail: Wrexham (free bus service to course – telephone above number for times)
By Air: Helicopter facilities

Bangor-on-Dee

2m 4f 110yds C
4m 1f C
2m 4f H

2m 1f H

2m 1f 110yds C
3m 6f C

BANGOR-ON-DEE

3m 110yds C
WP

3m H

3m 2f

BANGOR-ON-DEE: Plan of the course. This popular course, hardly a testing affair for the horses and riders, is where the author Dick Francis had his first racecourse ride.

Bath

The racecourse at Bath is situated to the north-west of the town, which can be conveniently reached by train from London Paddington, a mere 107 miles away. Special bus services from Bath and Bristol run to the track which is to be found at Lansdown on terrain that can usually be relied upon to produce good going. It is a left-handed oval of 1 mile 4 furlongs 25 yards in length.

The mile course, on which low-drawn horses enjoy an edge, starts from a spur which extends inside the main circuit, while yet another allows races of 1 mile 2 furlongs 46 yards, and 1 mile 3 furlongs 144 yards to be staged. Horses running over these two particular distances encounter some fairly extensive straight sections which are far from common on this sharp circuit.

Indeed, horses have to be able to negotiate its tight turns in order to stand a real chance in the longer races that are held at Bath. Even in sprint races, which are held over 5 furlongs 11 yards and 5 furlongs 161 yards, contestants encounter only a furlong or so of straight level

Bath Racecourse
Lansdown
Bath BA1 9BU
Tel: (01225) 424609
www.bath-racecourse.co.uk

HOW TO GET THERE:
From North: M5 (Junct. 15); M4 (Junct. 18); A46
From South: M5 (Junct. 15); M4 (Junct. 18)
From East: M4 (Junct. 18); A46
By Rail: Bath
By Air: Nearest facilities at Colerne or Bristol

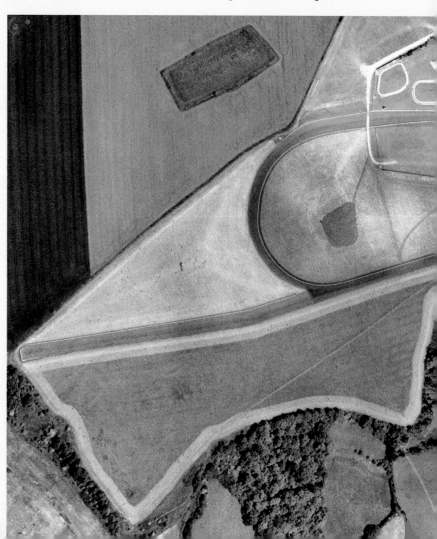

ground. Thereafter they have to descend and negotiate an elbow which, because it bends quite sharply to the left, gives an advantage to the low-drawn horses.

In view of the fact that all runners at Bath have to face this bend and encounter an uphill run-in that extends testingly for nearly half a mile, the Lansdown track, especially since its round sections are fairly undulating, can be regarded as tricky. Not only does it put a horse's speed, stamina, resolution and adaptability on trial, it also makes heavy demands on the skill of its rider. Horses need to be handily placed round its bends and if possible shot out of the elbow on the straight course. Thus, both adaptable galloping types and jockeys who have been conspicuously successful on this fairly lowly course should receive close scrutiny.

However, in view of the demanding, even bizarre, configuration of Bath racecourse, and the fact that the generally rather poor horses it attracts have to race at the unusually high altitude of 800 feet (which some believe accounts for so many freak results), the backer should perhaps avoid heavy investment at Lansdown.

BATH: Plan of the course.

Beverley

Beverley Racecourse
York Road
Beverley
East Yorkshire HU17 8QZ
Tel: (01482) 867488
www.beverley-racecourse.co.uk

HOW TO GET THERE:
From North: A1(M) (Junct. 47);
A54; A1079; A19 (from Thirsk)
From South: M1; A64
From East: A1035
From West: M62 (Junct. 37);
A614; A1079
By Rail: Beverley (approx. two miles)
By Air: Helicopter facilities

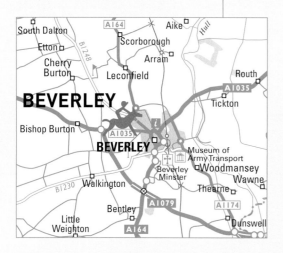

Beverley racecourse lies on common land known locally as the Westwood, a mile to the north-west of the town on the A1079 to York, and can be conveniently reached by motorway. The track itself extends for around 1 mile 3 furlongs and is stiff, egg-shaped and right-handed.

The 5-furlong course, which starts on a spur, features continuously rising ground. It also bends slightly to the right to join the round course after approximately 1½ furlongs. This confers an appreciable advantage on high-drawn sprinters, especially if the stalls are positioned on the far side. Since horses racing over the minimum trip at Beverley face a straight yet very testing uphill run-in of around 2½ furlongs, their claims should be considered only if no doubt whatsoever can be entertained about their stamina. Indeed, any first-season performer that is successful over Beverley's minimum distance, is likely to stay 6 furlongs on far easier courses.

Some moderately undulating ground is to be found on the round course. For example, horses run downhill round the penultimate bend and then travel uphill before entering the finishing straight. Significantly, it is on entering this that jockeys with sufficient experience of this demanding track can poach a lead which they have then to sustain over the punishing 3 furlongs and more that remain. Understandably then, Beverley is not really a suitable course for the adoption of waiting tactics. It would seem to suit long-striding gallopers that are sufficiently adaptable to race against the collar around its well-banked but fairly sharp right-handed turns and have sufficient resolution and courage. Since such a large proportion of the 7 furlong 100 yard course, the 1 mile 1 furlong 207 yard race distance, the 1 mile 4 furlong 16 yard course, and the stayers' distances of 2 miles 35 yards and 2 miles 3 furlongs involve right-hand bends, horses running on them which are highly drawn are distinctly favoured. Form students should give the claims of course and distance winners particular consideration.

An efficient watering system ensures that hard ground is seldom encountered; on the other hand, when the going at Beverley is soft it may pay to take a second look at any dour stayer that is known to be a confirmed 'mudlark'.

An excellent view is afforded of Beverley Minster which, along with the racing, is clearly visible from well-positioned grandstands.

BEVERLEY: Plan of the course. The Kiplingcotes Derby, said to be the the world's oldest horserace, was run in the region as early as 1519.

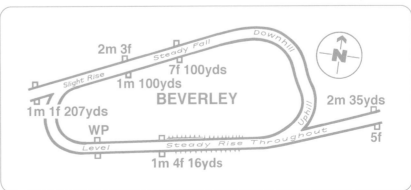

BEVERLEY

2m 3f
7f 100yds
1m 100yds
1m 1f 207yds
WP
1m 4f 16yds
2m 35yds
5f

Slight Rise
Steady Fall
Downhill
Uphill
Level
Steady Rise Throughout

Brighton

The Brighton track is to be found some 400 feet above sea level at Kemptown, two miles due east of this famous coastal town which benefits greatly from its excellent rail link with London some 53 miles away. It seems appropriate that so cosmopolitan a town has such a distinctive, pleasantly informal and quite spectacularly sited racecourse which is an essentially three-sided affair running round a downland shoulder that reminds many of its patrons of a rather singular horseshoe. This broad course is so undulating it is often likened to a switchback. It extends for 1½ miles and is rather reminiscent of the distinctive Epsom Derby course, since it bends quite sharply to the left and includes many severe gradients.

For these reasons, Brighton is a specialists' track. In fact, it tends to favour compact, well-made contestants that are sufficiently speedy to get quickly into their strides and make the running, and which are adaptable enough to remain sure-footed on its severely undulating terrain and fairly tight turns.

Brighton Racecourse
Freshfield Road
Brighton
East Sussex BN2 9XZ
Tel: (01273) 603580

HOW TO GET THERE:
From North: M23 (Junct. 11); A23
From East: A27
From West: A27
By Rail: Brighton (courtesy bus to course)
By Air: Shoreham Airport

The 1½ mile course actually extends for 1 mile 3 furlongs 196 yards and soon features ground that ascends to a sharp left-hand bend. A further uphill stretch is followed by a second, sharper left-hand turn that leads into the track's V-shaped top section, along which races are staged over 7 furlongs 214 yards, a slightly 'short' 6 furlongs and 5 furlongs 59 yards.

Sprinters need to be 'shot' from the stalls so as not to run wide as they plummet pell-mell round the course's final turn (whose negotiation can unbalance long-striding galloping types). This bend curves to the left, giving jockeys who have previously mastered Brighton's topographical idiosyncracies a valuable opportunity to poach an advantage of a length or two which they then have to try to maintain throughout the subsequent straight, yet undulating, 3½-furlong run-in. This continues to descend until the 2-furlong marker and then rises in a manner that is sufficiently steep to find out any

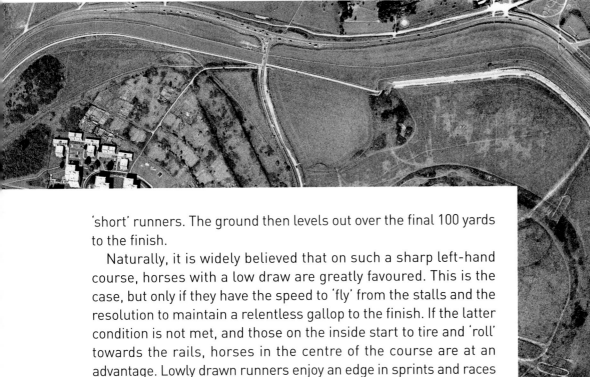

'short' runners. The ground then levels out over the final 100 yards to the finish.

Naturally, it is widely believed that on such a sharp left-hand course, horses with a low draw are greatly favoured. This is the case, but only if they have the speed to 'fly' from the stalls and the resolution to maintain a relentless gallop to the finish. If the latter condition is not met, and those on the inside start to tire and 'roll' towards the rails, horses in the centre of the course are at an advantage. Lowly drawn runners enjoy an edge in sprints and races run over 1 mile 1 furlong 209 yards and 1 mile 3 furlongs 196 yards.

Plan of the course.

Carlisle

Carlisle racecourse, situated some 300 miles from London, can be reached after leaving junction 42 of the M6 or after a rather spectacular run from Euston to Carlisle station, a mile away from the course. It is a pear-shaped, quite severely undulating affair which on the flat runs right-handed for just over a mile and a half. Runners over this particular distance start from a spur and first race right-handed and downhill for around 3 furlongs. Beyond the 1 mile 1 furlong 61 yards start they ascend as they approach the turn into the back straight along which sprints of 6 furlongs 206 yards are staged. Races over a 'short mile' of 7 furlongs 200 yards are started from a second spur at the top of the track.

After racing on the level back straight, runners in non-sprint races swing fairly sharply to the right before encountering a finishing stretch that features a testing 3½-furlong run-in whose steeply rising ground flattens out only 50 yards or so from the finish.

A spur that is perhaps more of a turning chute allows races to be run over 5 furlongs 193 yards and 5 furlongs. Horses tackling the latter trip find that it features two very different, if almost equal, sections of track. The first of these is a bend that for around 1½ furlongs turns to the right and then sweeps more gradually in this direction as it eventually joins the round course and enters the finishing straight; the second is the run-in itself which is fairly punishing, especially for two-year-olds whose claims should be seriously considered only if no doubts can be entertained about their stamina.

As for the draw, it is of little consequence in races run on the round course, but horses allotted high numbers in the sprint races are understandably favoured on this right-hand track when the stalls are positioned on the far side. However, the Carlisle course has a clay subsoil so soft ground conditions sometimes prevail, and in such a case low-drawn sprinters may for once enjoy an advantage, especially if they happen to be long-striding gallopers.

Horses tend to run well on this rather lowly but demanding course if they are ridden by jockeys who can bring them with well-timed runs, if they can adapt to the fairly easy right-hand bends and longish stretches of undulating ground that are found on the round course and if they have the finishing speed to sprint to the line over the last 50 yards of level ground.

Carlisle's picturesque setting in some of Cumbria's

Carlisle Racecourse
Durdar Road
Carlisle
Cumbria CA2 4TS
Tel: (01228) 522973
www.carlisle-races.co.uk

HOW TO GET THERE:
From North: A74(M); M6 (Junct. 42); A7 (from Hawick)
From South: M6 (Junct. 42)
From East: A69
From West: A596 (from Workington); A595 (from Whitehaven)
By Rail: Carlisle Citadel Station
By Air: Helicopter facilities

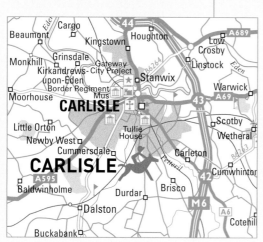

delightful lakeland also appeals to the jumping fraternity. The National Hunt track extends for 13 furlongs and is on the stiff side, not because of its nine birch fences faced with gorse, but because of the fact that severe undulations and an uphill finish of more than 250 yards mean that it takes some getting, especially when the going is heavy. This can often be the case in a wet winter in this never too dry part of the world.

CARLISLE: Plans of the Flat course (top), and the National Hunt course (bottom).

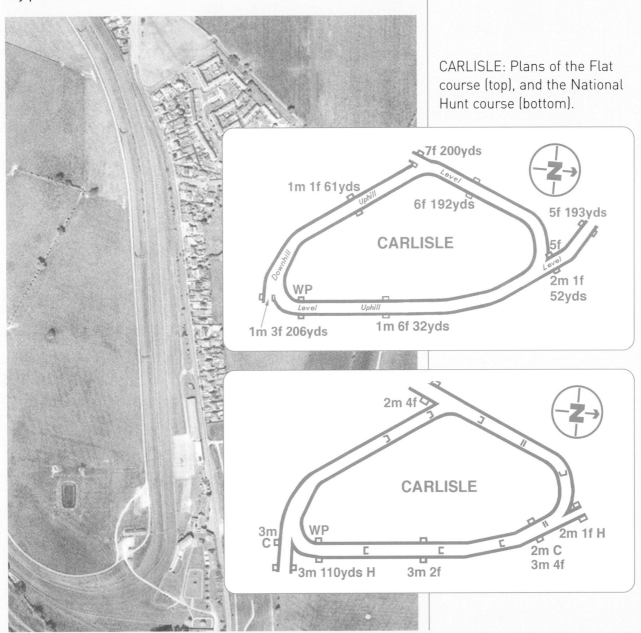

Carlisle

Carlisle

Cartmel

The victory at Cartmel on August Bank Holiday Monday in 1974 of Gay Future, the horse that featured in an attempt by its Irish connections to sting British bookmakers to the tune of £300,000, really placed this delightful Lake District jumping track on the racing map and was the main reason it now enjoys sophisticated links between the outside world and its betting shops such as telex and fax facilities, as well as racecourse telephones, whose absence in 1974 was the reason Cartmel was chosen for the Gay Future Coup.

Travellers to Cartmel can take the M6 and should leave it when they see Barrow-in-Furness signposted on the A590. The scenic last legs of the journey to the racecourse are well signposted by the AA. Rail passengers should alight at Cark & Cartmel, which is two and a half miles from the course, before taking a taxi, whilst any air travellers can consider the Ponderosa landing strip at nearby Flookburgh that forms part of Morecambe Bay.

As befits a track that stages many holiday meetings, the accent is on enjoyment. Indeed, so pleasant are Cartmel's sadly rather infrequent race days that if the weather is sufficiently enticing crowds of 10,000–20,000 flock to this picturesque playground where all the fun of the fair can be savoured.

Cartmel Racecourse
Cartmel
Nr. Grange-over-Sands
Cumbria LA11 6QF
Tel: (015395) 36340 (race days)
www.cartmel-
steeplechases.co.uk

HOW TO GET THERE:
From North: M6 (Junct. 36)
From South: M6 (Junct. 36); A590
From East: A65; A590
From West: A590
By Rail: Cark & Cartmel
By Air: Flookburgh; Helicopter facilities

Perhaps the sheer popularity of the track is the reason why no daily members' badges can be obtained. The drystone walls, the sight of a nearby priory and the trees and hills so beloved of the Lakeland poets remind some racegoers of many an Irish racecourse and give ballast to minds intent on winner finding – a process facilitated by the fact that pre-race parades are a popular course feature.

Six surprisingly stiff fences have to be

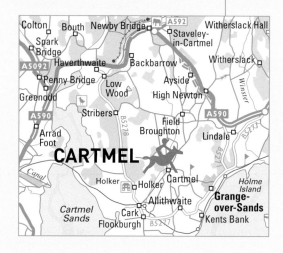

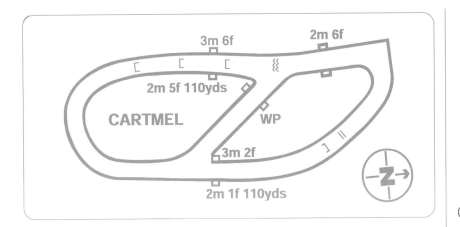

CARTMEL: Plan of the course.

negotiated at Cartmel, whose sharp circuit features slight undulations on the run-in which involves a chute in the middle of the track and can claim the distinction of being the longest in the country since it extends for around 800 yards. Before reaching the winning post the runners also have to cope with some slightly rising ground.

Cartmel's tight configuration and generally flat nature mean that it tends to suit nippy and handy types rather than dour long-striding stayers. Steeplechasers that have tackled 3 miles 2 furlongs have been spectacularly involved in three negotiations of a water jump on the back straight, while chasers are also faced with the rather rare race distance of 2 miles 5½ furlongs. All in all, Cartmel is a singular racecourse of considerable charm.

Catterick Bridge

Few seasoned racegoers are likely to cite Catterick Bridge as their favourite course, but it might well be so nominated by stable staff who appreciate the accommodation it offers them. Although some 244 miles from London and 5 miles south-east of picturesque Richmond, Catterick can be reached fairly conveniently by southern racegoers if they board Darlington-bound expresses at King's Cross. Many of those arriving by road take the A1 as the course lies to the east of this famous trunk road. The track itself, which is close to the major training centre of Middleham, is a sharp, cramped, oval circuit of 1 mile 198 yards. It favours front runners and short-striding contestants whose strong suit is speed rather than stamina. Indeed, horses can be 'kidded' into staying particular distances at Catterick that they would not be capable of getting on more testing tracks, especially if their jockeys are experienced enough to give them a flying start and keep them in handy positions throughout their races. Understandably, many previous winners over this rather singular course relish being back on its tight turns and thus acquit themselves well.

On the round course races are run over 7 furlongs, 1 mile 3 furlongs 214 yards, 1 mile 5 furlongs 175 yards, and 1 mile 7 furlongs 177 yards over ground that includes an uphill section beyond the winning post. One spur helps to provide a 7-furlong course on which runners initially race downhill, while the other allows 5-furlong sprints and contests over 1 mile 5 furlongs 175 yards to be staged. Runners in sprints run downhill for much of their journey.

Fast times are often set on the sprint course, the first 2 furlongs of which involve a fairly steep descent into a left-handed bend. The final 3 furlongs of the Catterick track make up a straight run-in which features slight undulations as it falls to the post and so increases the sprint course's suitability to short-running 'pigeon-catchers'!

Fortunately, soft or heavy ground is rare because the Catterick course has a fast-draining gravel subsoil that guarantees good natural drainage.

Racegoers are guaranteed an excellent view of the action at Catterick – a point not lost on National Hunt enthusiasts who congregate here in fair numbers during the winter months. The jumping track takes little getting, as its eight fences are hardly formidable affairs. It tends to suit small, handy, front-running speedsters that can poach leads around its tight turns that are long enough to

The Racecourse
Catterick Bridge
Richmond
North Yorkshire DL10 7PE
Tel: (01748) 811478
www.catterickbridge.co.uk

HOW TO GET THERE:
From North: A1(M)
From South: A1(M)
From East: A66 (from Middlesbrough)
From West: A66 (from Penrith)
By Rail: Darlington
By Air: R.A.F. Leeming

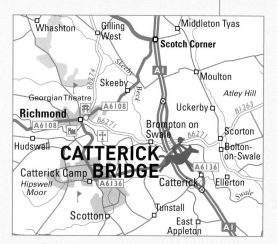

prevent their being pegged back on the short 240-yard run-in. Dour gallopers tend hardly to get going or to be able to stretch out and settle down on this rather workaday, although true spectator's, track. Previous course and distance winners should receive the close attention of form students.

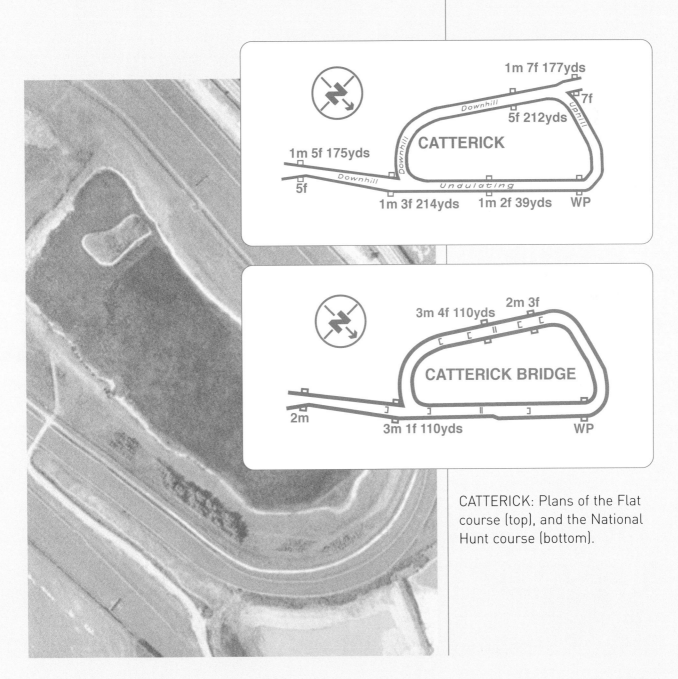

CATTERICK: Plans of the Flat course (top), and the National Hunt course (bottom).

Catterick Bridge

Cheltenham

Cheltenham Racecourse
Prestbury Park
Cheltenham
Gloucestershire GL50 4SH
Tel: (01242) 513014
www.cheltenham.co.uk

HOW TO GET THERE:
From North: M5 (Juncts. 9, 10);
A435
From South: M5 (Juncts. 10, 11)
From East: A40
From West: A40; M4 (Junct. 20);
M5 (Juncts. 10, 11)
By Rail: Cheltenham Spa
By Air: Helicopter facilities

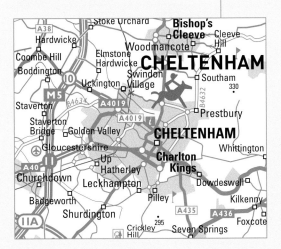

If asked to name their particular version of paradise, many racegoers would place Cheltenham's spectacularly amphitheatrical racecourse that nestles under Cleeve Hill high on their shortlist. Indeed, many superlatives have been lavished on this track which in the minds of many is quite simply the best steeplechase course this side of creation and which is unquestionably Britain's leading National Hunt racecourse. As the Irish would say, there is 'craic' aplenty to savour here, especially at the three-day Festival in March whose telling description as one of the 'rites of spring' testifies to its unparalleled splendour and firmly established place on the social calendar.

The course can be reached by rail from London Paddington via Cheltenham Spa whence special buses provide a shuttle service to the racecourse.

One measure of Cheltenham's excellence is that the majority of the jumping season's Grade One contests are staged upon it on one or other of two left-handed, oval-shaped and very undulating courses. The first of these, the so-called 'Old' course on which the Cheltenham Gold Cup was staged until 1958, extends for 1½ miles and involves nine formidable fences of which only one is found in the finishing straight. The Old course's final feature is a most testing uphill run-in of 350 yards that often proves the undoing of non-stayers lacking the courage and resolution that enabled the peerless Golden Miller to win five consecutive Gold Cups and so be commemorated by a splendid racecourse statue.

The slightly longer new circuit of ten fences follows the same route as its predecessor but leaves it after the seventh fence before again rejoining it after the tenth. On the new course the run-in is 237 yards long and a chute in the middle of the track allows hurdle races of 2 miles 5½ furlongs and chases of 2 miles 5 furlongs as well as 4 miles 1 furlong to be staged.

In the words of John Welcome, to act on this racecourse (since it provides a severe test of both its courage and conformation) 'a horse must be able to gallop, both up and downhill'. Cheltenham certainly takes some knowing and thus past course winners, partnered by jockeys with high 'wins to mounts' ratios, should receive special attention. Countless races have been lost at Cheltenham at the third last fence, often by jockeys on heavily backed contenders driving their mounts too hard as they race downhill to this

Cheltenham

Opposite: Cheltenham, quite simply the best steeplechase course this side of creation.

obstacle so that these crash out of contention or slip up on its landing side.

For many racing enthusiasts the best way to begin the New Year is to attend Cheltenham's two-day fixture that always takes place before and over that Bank Holiday. Another January fixture is staged at the end of the month and acts as a curtain-raiser to The Festival itself. The latter is so famous and popular that, as the course brochure puts it, the 'whole world of steeplechasing descends on the elegant spa town of Cheltenham'. The 20 races staged during The Festival offer prize money well in excess of £2 million.

By tradition the meeting opens with the 2 mile 110 yards Supreme Novices Hurdle, a highly competitive affair that always attracts a huge field. Also staged on the opening day is the Arkle Challenge Trophy, a 16-furlong 'chase for future champions, run to commemorate the best post-war 'chaser to have won the Cheltenham Gold Cup and so deserve the tribute of a racecourse statue.

CHELTENHAM: Plan of the New course.

CHELTENHAM
(New Course)

2m 5f 110yds H
2m 5f C
4m 1f C
2m 4f 110yds H
3m H
2m 1f H
2m 110yds C
3m 4f 110yds C
3m 2f 110yds C
3m 1f 110yds C
WP

The highlight of The Festival's opening card is, of course, the Champion Hurdle and here it may pay backers to be mindful of the multiple successes of several horses that the past results of this matchless contest so prominently feature. Interestingly, Dawn Run was not one of these but, of course, achieved fame, and is commemorated in bronze, as the first horse to win both the Champion Hurdle (in 1984) and the Gold Cup two years later.

Wednesday's centrepiece is the 2-mile Queen Mother Champion Chase, which commemorates steeplechasing's late, most sporting and popular owner. This is often won by a past winner and is not usually a race for outsiders.

The final 'chase on the second day of The Festival commemorates Lord Mildmay, undoubtedly the unluckiest jockey in Grand National history, and another of steeplechasing's most sporting owners, prior to his tragic death by drowning. The Mildmay of Flete Challenge Cup is a handicap 'chase of 2 miles 4½ furlongs.

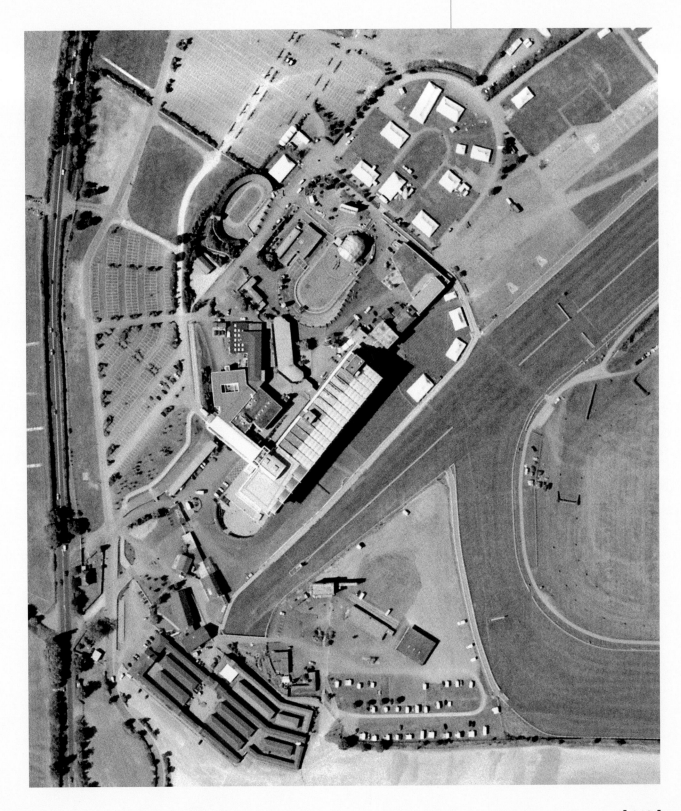

Cheltenham

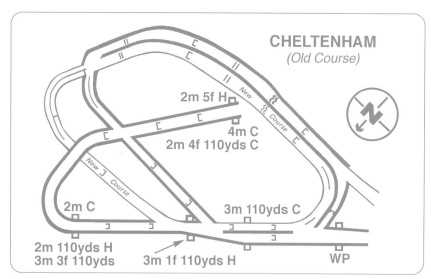

CHELTENHAM: Plan of the Old course.

The Triumph Hurdle, the curtain-raiser to The Festival's final day, is a race that is now attracting, and has recently been won by, runners from top flat-racing stables. The Stayers' Hurdle of 3 miles ½ furlong is on occasion won by a past winner.

Next comes the highlight of the entire festival, the Cheltenham Gold Cup. This, the 'blue riband' and championship of steeplechasing, is the race in which, despite the odd upset (like Norton's Coin at 100–1 in 1990), form tends to work out well. Past winners sometimes register repeat victories in this race.

While on three magical days in March championship races are staged for each type of horse involved in National Hunt racing – there is now even a Festival Bumper – on other racing days, many other fine races are also staged at Cheltenham. The most prestigious is a handicap steeplechase of 2 miles 4½ furlongs that takes place early in November, which for many past years was sponsored by drinks' manufacturers.

On one of two other so-called 'premier days' – a Saturday in early December – the Tripleprint Gold Cup Handicap Chase is run over the same distance.

The Cheltenham season always closes with an idyllic fixture that to steeplechasing's cognoscenti is pure magic – the hunters' meeting that always takes place on the last Wednesday evening in April and attracts a most colourful cross-section of English sporting society from the shires. One race on this card, the 4 mile 1 furlong Hunters' Steeplechase, often provides a thrilling finish.

A cross-country chase course was established in 1995. On this, races reminiscent of steeplechasing's rustic and Corinthian origins provide a thrilling sight for spectators.

Chepstow

Chepstow Racecourse
Chepstow
Monmouthshire NP16 6BE
Tel: (01291) 622260
www.chepstow-racecourse.co.uk

HOW TO GET THERE:
From North: M5 (Junct. 15); M48
(Junct. 2)
From South: M5 (Junct. 15); M48
(Junct. 2)
From East: M4 (Junct. 4); M48
(Junct. 2)
From West: M4 (Junct. 23); M48
(Junct. 2)
By Rail: Chepstow
By Air: Helicopter facilities

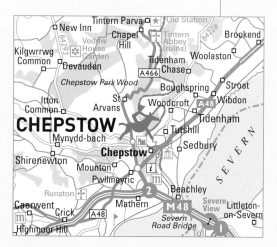

Located 135 miles from London, Chepstow racecourse, established in 1926, is the most recently constructed of British turf racecourses and offers a large number of fixtures. It forms part of Piercefield Park, a most picturesque stretch of undulating wooded parkland that can be reached after a two-to three-minute drive northwards from the Welsh side of the Severn Bridge. Its position, two miles away from the M48, makes it particularly accessible for racegoers.

It can also be reached by train from Paddington station via either Bristol Parkway or Newport stations.

The track used for flat racing is a left-handed oval which, although it has an extensive circumference of almost two miles, does not suit every strong, long-striding galloper, since its pronounced undulations include some quite severe and tricky gradients. However, a horse that has courage and sufficient stamina should not be unduly inconvenienced, especially if it is sufficiently adaptable to avoid becoming unbalanced as it negotiates the switchbacks and the sharp left-hand turns on the round course.

The straight 1 mile 14 yard course (along which starting stalls are also placed at around 7, 6 and 5 furlongs) initially runs downhill, joins the round course just after 3 furlongs and then begins to undulate. It rises sharply for two furlongs or so and then further major undulations are encountered before the finishing line is reached.

Most judges maintain that on the straight course, high-drawn horses have the edge especially when the stalls are positioned on the stands side and the going is anything but soft or heavy, while on the round course (as is to be expected on a left-hand track) those drawn low nearest the inside rail are favoured in races over 10 furlongs 36 yards, 12 furlongs 23 yards, 2 miles 49 yards, and 18 furlongs.

Since the subsoil of the straight course consists of clay, heavy going can sometimes chop the speed of sprinters and milers and put their stamina fully on trial.

Chepstow's near 5-furlong run-in gives patient jockeys riding in the longer races the opportunity to come gradually from behind and wear down the opposition.

The flat course was initially dubbed the 'Goodwood of the West' and to many this seems justified by a real attendance growth of 19 per cent in paying visitors in 2002 over 2001.

Chepstow is also remembered as the track on which Sir

Gordon Richards went through the card on 4 October 1933 and then, on the following day, won the first five races. This remarkable achievement is commemorated by the staging of the Sir Gordon Richards Stakes at an evening meeting in July.

In 2003 the flat-racing programme was significantly upgraded with the inclusion of the Group Three Golden Daffodil Stakes, and a new £20,000 pattern race staged in June.

Chepstow is also a Grade One National Hunt course (of, in essence, two long straights, two tight turns and 11 fences) and has many feature races including the Rehearsal Chase, Persian War Novices' Hurdle, the Tote Silver Trophy and Rising Stars Novices' Chase, with the £80,000 Coral Welsh National being the jewel in the crown. The sight at Chepstow of steeplechasers (especially those contesting the 3 miles 5½ furlong Welsh National in late December) against the course's sylvan backcloth, is both stirring and picturesque. The Welsh National frequently falls to a far from over-burdened, but improving, seven-year-old staying 'chaser and in its time has often been farmed by one or two particular trainers.

There has been significant investment in facilities at Chepstow, that is now in the midst of a £10.3 million redevelopment. A new paddock complex, an owners' and trainers' bar with viewing balcony and terrace, a premier stand with annual members' bar and new corporate boxes are already completed and in use. The whole scheme will be finished in 2006.

CHEPSTOW: Plans of the Flat course (top), and the National Hunt course (bottom).

Chepstow is the most recently constructed turf racecourse in Britain.

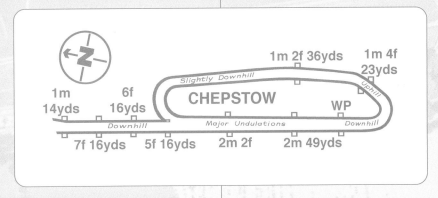

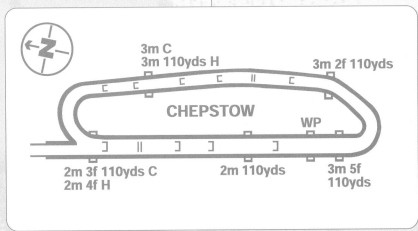

Chepstow

Chepstow

Chester

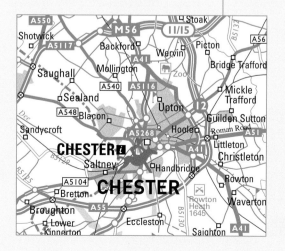

Chester Racecourse
Chester CH1 2LY
Tel: (01244) 304600
www.chester-races.co.uk

HOW TO GET THERE:
From North: M6 (Junct. 20); M56 (Junct. 15); M53 (Junct. 12)
From South: M6 (Junct. 20); M56 (Junct. 15); A41 (from Whitchurch); A483 (from Wrexham)
From East: A51 (from Nantwich); M56 (Junct. 15)
From West: A55 (from Colwyn Bay); A494 (from Ruthin)
By Rail: Chester General
By Air: Helicopter facilities

The ancient racecourse of Chester, on which racing took place for a silver bell as early as 1541, is situated close to the River Dee and is bounded by part of a Roman city wall. It is three-quarters of a mile from Chester's mainline station which can be conveniently reached from London Euston some 180 miles or so away. It is the smallest and tightest track in Britain. Indeed, in constituting what is almost a continuous and extremely sharp left-handed turn, it reminds many racegoers of a saucer or a site for chariot racing.

The track itself, which is flat throughout, extends for a mere mile and around 60 yards and thus does not give large, galloping types a chance to get into their long strides. Indeed, such animals often become unbalanced or run wide round Chester's sharp left-handed bends. These naturally tend to be appreciated by small or medium-sized horses that are sharp-actioned and sufficiently speedy to fly from the stalls. Front runners and horses that like to lie up with leaders often do well on this singular track as, understandably, do previous course winners or 'Chester specialists'.

The longest races on the 'Roodeye', and the only ones in which it is really possible to ride a waiting race, are staged over what can amount to a rather gruelling 2 miles 2 furlongs 147 yards in the course of which the runners pass the stands on three separate occasions! A famous event run over this marathon distance is the Chester Cup, first staged in 1824, which, while not a Group race, invariably provides a thrilling spectacle and, since it is run at such a blistering pace throughout, makes considerable demands on stamina. The Cup is always a major betting race at the prestigious three-day May meeting and in the nineteenth century ranked second only to the Derby in the ante-post wagering it attracted.

Another prestigious race is the Group Three Chester Vase run over 1 mile 4 furlongs 66 yards. First run in 1907, this event, since it tests the adaptability of Epsom hopefuls, is rightly regarded as a Derby trial.

Chester's other Group race, the Ormonde Stakes, is named after the unbeaten Triple Crown winner of 1886. A weight-for-age contest of 1 mile 5 furlongs 89 yards, it frequently falls to a four-year-old – sometimes to one as illustrious as Derby winner Teenoso, who captured it in 1984.

It has been estimated that the services of a jockey who can get his mount to put its near fore forward and go the 'shortest way round' are equivalent to a 7 lb pull in the weights. Above all, jockeys must be in contention as they round the final bend at Chester if their mounts are to stand any chance of reaching the frame, since the run-in of only 230 yards – the shortest of any British track – is insufficient for the making of any really significant late headway.

A low draw in sprint events, especially when the stalls are placed near the inside rail, is worth several pounds, and can sometimes prove the decisive factor.

The going is often good on this delightful Cheshire course where races are usually truly run. Chester, above all, provides spectacular viewing since its tightness and walled-in nature gives the impression that racehorses run faster here than anywhere else in Britain. That minority of runners known to appreciate its configuration may again do so!

CHESTER: Plan of the course.

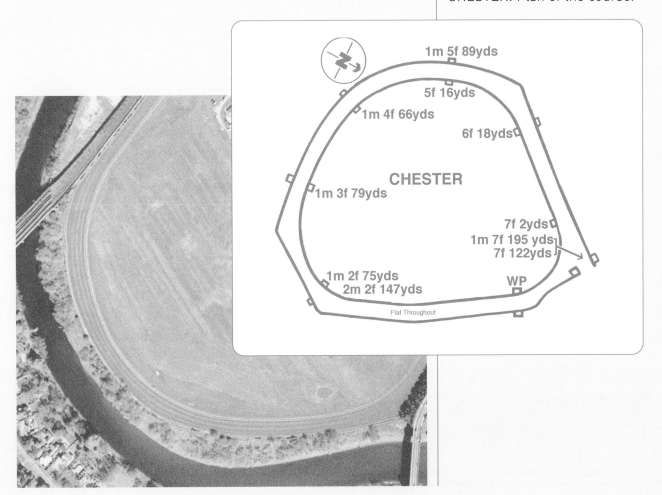

1m 5f 89yds
5f 16yds
1m 4f 66yds
6f 18yds
CHESTER
1m 3f 79yds
7f 2yds
1m 7f 195 yds
7f 122yds
1m 2f 75yds
2m 2f 147yds
WP
Flat Throughout

Chester

Curragh, The

The Curragh Racecourse
Co. Kildare
Ireland
Tel: +353 (0)45 441205
www.curragh.ie

HOW TO GET THERE:
From North: N80
From South: N9
From East: N7
From West: N7
By Rail: Curragh Mainline
By Air: Helicopter facilities

Cross-country horseracing originally formed a part of many a fair or 'oenach' (one of whose meanings is the 'contention of horses') and one well-known such event was held at the Cuireach (Curragh/racecourse) of Kildare where contests, and sometimes chariot races, took place involving horses (many imported from Wales) that were ridden by noblemen's sons and the red branch knights of pre-Christian Ireland.

Races have thus been staged for centuries on the vast grassy limestone plain that, appropriately, is the home of all five Irish Classic races and the headquarters of the Irish Turf Club and National Hunt Committee, and is therefore Ireland's equivalent to Newmarket.

As is the case with the Suffolk town, the Curragh has attracted a nearby National Stud as well as a sizeable cluster of prominent stud farms and racing stables run by trainers who take advantage of the local turf, a unique combination of red fescue and brown bent grass, ideally suited to the galloping of racehorses.

The course itself is a horseshoe-shaped, right-handed affair whose lack of severe undulations, sharp bends and any marked topographic eccentricity makes it a very fair test of the thoroughbred.

This track extends for around 2 miles and on its straight course races are staged over 5 furlongs and, thanks to a dog-leg of a spur, also over 6 furlongs, 6 furlongs 63 yards and over 7, 8 and 9 furlongs. Races are also run over 2 miles, 14 furlongs, 1½ miles, 10 furlongs and a 'round' mile. The Irish Derby course is regarded by many as a demanding test, far superior to, and fairer than, the Epsom Derby course.

As for the draw, it is generally held that it has no marked effect, except on the round course on which low-drawn horses may be at a slight advantage.

The track can be reached directly by helicopter and (on race days only) in trains that make a 40-minute non-stop run from Dublin's Heuston station to Curragh Mainline which conveniently is a mere 500 yards from the stands.

Those travelling by road can approach the course on some extremely scenic routes and will find it is some 29 miles south-west of Dublin. The course enclosures, most commendably, are combined into one area, save on Group One days and Irish Derby day which is now a Sunday in late June or early July.

As is appropriate for Ireland's showpiece track, the Curragh has excellent amenities including a completely covered tote area and seats reservable on a daily basis (for which tickets can be obtained at the racecourse office by the parade ring). Fruit is even on sale and hot table d'hôte luncheons are available in the first floor restaurant area above the tote hall in the grandstand, which also includes an enticing panoramic bar and a novel fish and tea bar. There is even a pub under the grandstand.

Children are extremely well catered for at the Curragh, in a leisureplex playground at the western end of the grandstand.

The richest pickings on offer at the Curragh are naturally the Irish Derby, the Irish Oaks, 2000 Guineas, 1000 Guineas and the St Leger, while the 7-furlong National Stakes staged in mid-September is a most prestigious race for first-season performers, as is the Phoenix Stakes run in early August. The very first two runnings of the Irish Derby, in the 1860s, went to English raiders, thereby establishing a trend that modern-day handlers like Michael Stoute have sometimes followed. Another top-class Curragh race is the Moyglare Stud Stakes for two-year-olds, which is the highlight of a Sunday card in late August or early September. The Irish Lincoln run in the spring and the Irish Cambridgeshire and Cesarewitch in the autumn are always exciting races on which fortunes can be wagered.

As befits a course so steeped in tradition, the Curragh stages several races that commemorate past champions. Thus, the Gladness Stakes, run in early to mid-April, recalls the horse that won the Ascot Gold Cup, the Goodwood Cup and the Ebor Handicap at York.

The Tetrarch Stakes, run at the end of April, is named after the horse one noted judge has described as 'unquestionably one of the most remarkable ever seen on the turf and possibly the fastest', while Pretty Polly, a filly that captured the English Triple Crown in 1904, is commemorated in Group races run in midsummer and late July.

THE CURRAGH: Plan and view of the course.

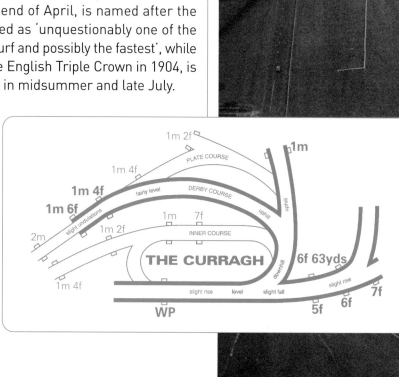

Doncaster

Doncaster's Group One racecourse, some 160 miles from London, can be reached by rail from King's Cross (arrive Doncaster Central) or via the A1(M) and the M18 and M180.

It is perhaps appropriate that its postal address is Leger Way, since Town Moor is the home of Britain's oldest Classic, run over a distance of 1 mile 6 furlongs 132 yards, that almost constitutes a complete circuit of this largely flat, 15½-furlong left-handed course which seems to favour long-striding galloping types with a turn of foot, the performers to which the 4½-furlong run-in is particularly suited. The round course, shaped like a cone or pear, and whose only undulations are provided by a small hill some 10 furlongs from the finish, is used for some races over 1 mile, for events over 1 mile 2 furlongs 60 yards, 1½ miles and 2¼ miles, as well as for contests over the St Leger distance. The course only turns to the left in a most accommodating, gently sweeping fashion. Lowly drawn contestants enjoy an advantage only in races from 8 to 12 furlongs run on the round course which in modern times has been used to stage the Lincoln Handicap on only one occasion (in 1978).

Horses tackling the round mile start from a short spur and then sweep left-handed before joining the finishing straight which forms the final section of the very wide straight mile course that is partly provided by a second spur.

Since the draw on Doncaster's straight course can prove crucial to high-drawn runners, it is imperative that a jockey is sufficiently experienced either to profit greatly from a favoured stalls position or to overcome a poor draw.

The turf on Town Moor provides some of the best racing ground in the country and sticky conditions are usually precluded by its sandy subsoil.

The Group One St Leger is contested early in September. This, the oldest of the Classics, was first run four years before the Derby in 1776 to commemorate Lt-Gen. Anthony St Leger (originally pronounced 'Sellinger'), a resident of Park Hill, which gives its name to another race for three-year-old fillies that is also run over the same distance each September.

One of the biggest nineteenth-century St Leger coups concerned Elis, whose owner Lord George Bentinck hit upon the ingenious idea of running this 1835 Molecomb Stakes winner so frequently in the south during the summer of the following year that few would feel he was

Doncaster Racecourse
The Grandstand
Leger Way
Doncaster DN2 6BB
Tel: (01302) 304207
www.doncaster-racecourse.com

HOW TO GET THERE:
From North: A1(M) (Junct. 35); M18 (Junct. 3); A368
From South: M1; M18 (Junct. 3); A368
From East: M180 (Junct. 1)
From West: A635; M62 (Junct. 35); M18 (Junct. 3); A368
By Rail: Doncaster
By Air: Helicopter facilities, Doncaster Airport

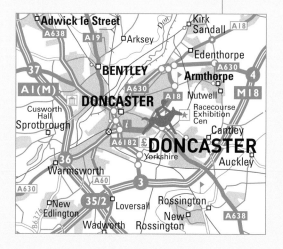

likely to line up for the St Leger after walking all the way to Doncaster from his Goodwood stable. However, Elis was spirited northwards in a horse van drawn by four other horses – a virtually unprecedented ploy – and he duly landed the Leger at 7–2.

Gladiateur in 1866 was an even more widely travelled French winner, while Ormonde, Persimmon and Nijinsky are just three other Derby winners to have prevailed at Doncaster to perhaps prove the adage that 'while the fittest horse wins the 2000 Guineas and the luckiest horse wins the Derby, the best horse wins the St Leger'.

This race is the highlight of Doncaster's most prestigious four-day September fixture, a major attraction of which is the May Hill Stakes, a mile race for first-season fillies, first run in 1981. Also staged at this meeting are the prestigious Park Hill Stakes and the Doncaster Cup, an often thrilling marathon which has most frequently fallen to a four-year-old.

As for the Champagne Stakes, this is a top-class 7-furlong contest for two-year-old colts and geldings.

Yet another feature of the four-day September fixture is the Flying Childers Stakes, a 5-furlong race for two-year-olds that commemorates the so-called 'first great racehorse', which was foaled in 1715.

Late in the autumn, a most prestigious Group One mile race for two-year-olds, the Racing Post Trophy, is staged. Infrequently won by a horse destined for Classic success, it nevertheless attracts

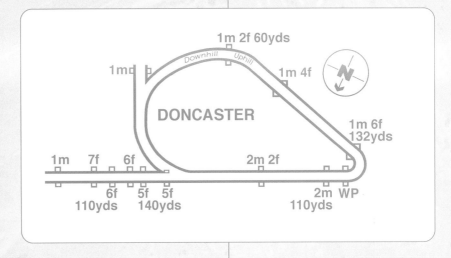

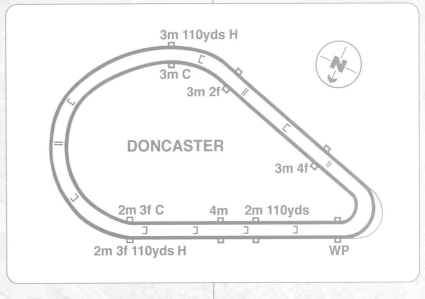

DONCASTER: Plans of the Flat course (top) over which the St Leger is run, and of the National Hunt course (bottom).

Doncaster

first-season performers of the highest calibre.

By tradition, Doncaster fixtures in March and November have opened and closed the turf flat-racing season, most spectacularly via the Lincoln and November Handicaps. These are major lotteries, as the victory in the latter of Tearaway at 40–1 in 1955 aptly confirmed. In recent runnings of the Lincoln Handicap, four-year-olds have faired slightly better than five-year-olds, while the 'November' is often lifted by a late improving three-year-old.

Doncaster's jumping track has fair fences and, like the flat course, tends to suit long-striding gallopers. Its best-known jump race is the Great Yorkshire Chase, a 3-mile event staged late in January. The Freebooter Novices Chase run in early December commemorates the 1950 Yorkshire-trained winner of the Grand National.

This historic racecourse remains in racing's first division.

Epsom Downs

Epsom Downs Racecourse
Surrey KT18 5LQ
Tel: (01372) 726311
www.epsomderby.co.uk

HOW TO GET THERE:
From North: M1 (Junct. 6A); M25 (Junct. 8); A217
From South: M23 (Junct. 8); M25 (Junct. 8); A217
From East: M25 (Junct. 8); A217; M20 (Junct. 3); M26
From West: M3 (Junct. 2); M25 (Junct. 8)
By Rail: Epsom; Epsom Downs; Tattenham Corner
By Air: Helicopter facilities

Epsom Downs racecourse, a mere 17 miles from central London, is readily accessible by road or rail, there being no fewer than three nearby stations. It is the home of the Derby, arguably the most famous horserace in the world and, in the view of Hugh McIlvanney, 'one of the last genuine folk festivals left to us', which came into being in a rather bizarre fashion in 1779 when Sir Charles Bunbury lost the toss of a sovereign to the 12th Earl of Derby and so forfeited his right to name a new mile race for three-year-old colts.

The two aristocrats felt that such an event would provide a fitting companion for the Oaks – a 12-furlong race for three-year-old fillies, named after the hunting lodge of Lord Derby – and won for this true child of fortune by his filly Bridget on its inaugural running in 1779. As for the Derby, justice was finally dispensed when Sir Charles Bunbury's Diomed ran out its first winner in 1780 at 6–4. Lord Derby himself had to wait until 1787 when another 'aristocrat', Sir Peter Teazle, a horse he had named to honour his second wife, triumphed at 2–1.

There were perhaps two main reasons why the Derby and the Oaks caused such an initial stir and were beginning to alert far-seeing entrepreneurs to their commercial potential by the time the latter event had been run for the first time as a 12-furlong affair in 1784. Firstly, they featured no preliminary heats which, until Lt-Gen. Anthony's St Leger's innovation at Doncaster in 1776, had represented the standard way in which races were decided on the English turf. The Derby and the Oaks thus accelerated the change towards the modern practice of deciding races at one running. Secondly, the colts' Classic was given the ultimate accolade when Disraeli called to mind a part of the insignia of the Order of the Garter in describing the Derby as the 'blue ribbon' (riband) of the turf. The occasional criticisms that have over the years been made of the Epsom Derby have mainly stemmed from disquiet that the world's best-known race is run over such a singular 12-furlong course. That this, in fact, poses a threat to the valuable thoroughbreds that race upon it, is a belief that to some the full catalogue of recent Derby catastrophes would seem to justify. For example, despite storming home in the 1980 Derby, Henbit was found to have cracked a cannon bone in his off-fore. Tragically, this injury prevented him from ever again distinguishing himself on the racecourse. Such accidents should, however, be placed in perspective and be seen as

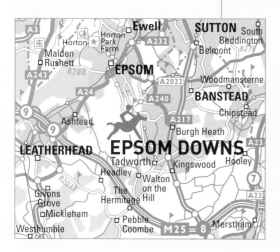

the penalty that some horses with less than perfect conformation occasionally have to pay if they fail Epsom's searching test or meet with ill-luck in running. The risk that their charges may sustain injury in a race in which some jockeys abandon their customary caution and ride at a dangerously wild pace on constantly changing gradients, may deter a few owners from letting their horses take their chances. However, the Derby still deserves Disraeli's eulogy.

A Derby winner can bring a fortune in stud fees to its owner. Shergar, for example, the ill-fated 1981 winner, was syndicated for £10 million.

The present Derby course was first used in 1872, after complaints were finally heeded that the steep 1-in-18 gradient in the first 500 yards of the new 1848 course influenced results to a disproportionate extent.

EPSOM DOWNS: Plan of the course

Contestants tackling 1½ miles and (as discovered in 1991) 10 yards at Epsom initially encounter ground that rises quite steeply and then turns appreciably to the right. By the time it enters the section that runs past the mile post, the Derby field has raced round something of a dog leg. With just under a mile to run, at a point where again a road traverses the course, the track starts to swing quite sharply to the left. It also continues to rise,

but in a more gradual, if uneven, manner. At the top of the hill, some 166 yards short of the halfway mark at the 6-furlong pole, the Derby runners meet ground that is 134 feet higher than that at the start and then race on a level stretch of almost 300 yards, that includes quite a large part of this first left-hand bend which is longer and rather more gradual than its sharp successor at Tattenham Corner. This famous feature of the Derby course used to be far sharper prior to its alteration earlier this century and is preceded by a steep descent of 40 feet in 300 yards, which has proved the undoing of so many ungainly Derby runners. After Tattenham Corner comes the run-in of just under 4 furlongs, the ground continuing to fall, but at a gradually decreasing rate until a mere 100 yards remain.

It is form this position well inside the crucial final furlong that the ground appears to rise steadily to the winning post. This is, in fact, an optical illusion under which tiring Epsom finishers, quite as much as a whole host of turf writers, have plainly laboured. As the Ordnance Survey map confirms, the ground is practically flat. A thorough survey carried out in 1980 shows a rise of barely three feet over 100 yards. Even more surprising is the fact, pointed out by Mr T. P. Neligan, when Managing Director of former owners United Racecourses Limited, that, as the winning post the ground slopes away from the stand very sharply – by five feet in fact across the course – a horse rounding Tattenham Corner, crossing over to the stands side and then gradually back towards the winning post on the far side, could probably maintain a downhill momentum all the way!

All in all, although Epsom is not really a testing track, its 12 furlong 10 yard course does impose a true test of stamina. The initial uphill section is taken at a taxing pace which saps the strength of non-stayers and leaves them with little in reserve by the time they face the long run-in. As well as making demands on the stamina, courage and resolution of its contestants, the brisk pace of the Derby puts their speed on trial.

Perhaps the heaviest demands the Derby makes are on the adaptability of those taking part. As John Hislop has stated so succinctly, 'the perfect Derby horse must be able to race smoothly and effectively under a number of distinctive and different circumstances'. So an almost flawless conformation is required.

Below: Epsom Downs: home to the Derby – 'one of the last genuine folk festivals left to us'.

Indeed, it is rare that a Derby winner's physical make-up can be seriously faulted.

Despite its difficulties and the significant fact that only the very best of jockeys, like Steve Donoghue and Lester Piggott, have been described as 'Derby specialists', the course should not present accomplished jockeys with any serious difficulty. Apart from ensuring that their mounts are not asked to tackle the initial uphill stretch at too taxing an early pace, jockeys should take them the shortest way over its first 4 furlongs. For low-drawn horses, this entails tacking over from the inside rails towards the far rails at the 1 mile 2 furlong gate and then moving smartly back again to regain an inside berth in time to save ground around the first long left-hand bend. As for Tattenham Corner, most jockeys like to be lying 'handy' as it is negotiated, although many a Derby has been won by a horse that has appeared hopelessly boxed-in or too far behind at this particular point. On the run-in itself, it is vital that horses are kept balanced as they descend ground that slopes from left to right towards the inside running rail. The centre of the course is the ideal position, since it gives the jockey clear ground from which he can deliver his final challenge, as Lester Piggott demonstrated to such good effect on his very first Derby winner, Never Say Die, in 1954.

Above: Tattenham Corner. It was here that suffragette Emily Davidson died after throwing herself into the path of King George V's runner in the 1913 Derby. After rounding this famous course feature, the ill-fated Shergar went on to win the 1981 Derby by a record 10 lengths.

Epsom was once associated with other well-known races which sadly have now lost not just the kudos they enjoyed long before many major flat races were 'listed' or given 'pattern' status, but their very existence. One such event was the Great Metropolitan Handicap, first run in 1846 over Epsom's now-defunct, perhaps even eccentric 2 mile 2 furlong 'Great Metropolitan' course, which started just beyond the winning post in front of the stands. This race was once popularly known as the Publicans' Derby. Another once well-known Epsom race that has also been lost is the 1 mile 2 furlong City and Suburban Handicap, first run in 1851.

Epsom Downs

Events run over 7 and 6 furlongs at Epsom are started from short spurs which soon lead into the round course, while races over 5 furlongs are staged on the 'Egmont' course which, for Epsom, is unusually straight. The belief that this is the world's fastest sprint course is strengthened by the face that the fastest time every recorded over 5 furlongs was clocked by Indigenous, a four-year-old who humped no less than 9 st 5 lb to victory on firm going at the 1960 Derby meeting at an average speed of 41.98 mph.

All events run over the minimum distance at Epsom start from a third spur after which comes a 4-furlong run-in. Not surprisingly, sprinters that can fly from the stalls and continue to make the running at a relentless gallop are at an advantage, as the track they race on is almost all downhill, although it is possible for a horse to win if it is brought from behind by an experienced jockey who is a good judge of pace.

At Epsom, with the stalls in any position, high-drawn horses, if they have the speed to fly from the gate and maintain a fast pace, are favoured in sprints. The going at Epsom often remains good or good to firm as the track has a chalky subsoil. In longer events, the acquisition and retention by jockeys of ideal places from which to deliver effective challenges is far more crucial than the allocation of any particular position in the draw.

As for other prestigious races staged at Epsom, the Group One Coronation Cup, run over the full Derby distance, is often captured by a (sometimes French) four-year-old middle-distance performer in peak form, while two other notable events are staged at the June meeting, the Diomed Stakes (run to commemorate the winner of the first Derby) over 1 mile 114 yards and the Northern Dancer Stakes, a 12 furlong 10 yard handicap run in memory of the sire of such Derby winners as Nijinsky, The Minstrel and Secreto.

Exeter

Exeter's fixtures are actually staged at Haldon in a rural and picturesque setting on the fringes of Dartmoor's forestland. The extensive right-handed, oval-shaped track that runs through gorse and heather is close to the A38 Plymouth to Exeter road and is six miles west of the latter town, whose airport can accommodate airborne racegoers arriving in fixed-wing aircraft. Helicopters can land (by prior arrangement) at the Racecourse itself. Rail travellers should alight at Exeter St Davids which can be reached after a fairly fast journey of less than 200 miles from London Paddington.

The A38 is the route from the west to Exeter Racecourse on top of Haldon Hill, while those coming from Plymouth should take the A38. The Exeter–Plymouth bus service will drop you at the racecourse.

Most appropriately, the William Hill Haldon Gold Cup is the most prestigious race (since listed) that takes place on this rather hilly track, whose often quite severe gradients mean that past course and distance runners should be respected. Such runners are unlikely to be long-striding gallopers who often find this course's gradients and undulations rather unsettling. The uphill run-in is 300 yards long.

The likes of Desert Orchid and Best Mate won their first races at Exeter and the course suggests visiting Exeter 'to see tomorrow's Champions today.'

Exeter Racecourse
Kennford
Exeter
Devon EX6 7XS
Tel: (01392) 832599
www.exeter-racecourse.co.uk

HOW TO GET THERE:
From North: M5 (Junct. 31 at end); A38
From South: A38
From East: A5; M5 (Junct. 31); A38
From West: A30 from Okehampton
By Rail: Exeter St Davids
By Air: Exeter Airport; Helicopter facilities

EXETER: Plan of the course.

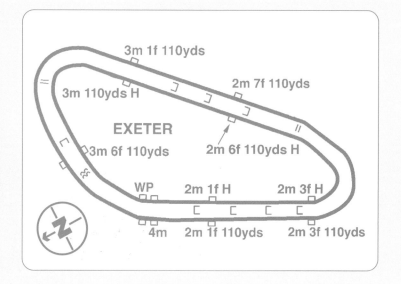

Fakenham

Fakenham Racecourse
Fakenham
Norfolk NR21 7NY
Tel: (01328) 862388
www.fakenhamracecourse.co.uk

HOW TO GET THERE:
From North: B1105 (from Wells-next-the-Sea)
From South: A1065 (from Swaffham)
From East: A1067 (from Norwich); A148 (from Cromer)
From West: A148 (from King's Lynn)
By Rail: King's Lynn (22 miles)
By Air: Helicopter facilities

The fixtures staged on this East Anglian country course, although fairly minor, are friendly sporting affairs, especially if the weather is fine enough to have a picnic in the course enclosure. The rural setting and simple charm of Fakenham create a unique and convivial atmosphere.

As is appropriate on a course on which so many hunters' races are staged, something of a point-to-point atmosphere prevails at Fakenham, whose proximity to Sandringham is the reason why the Prince of Wales' Cup and the Queen's Cup are two prestigious races that are contested here each season. The royal connections extend still further as in 1886, the West Norfolk Hunt – which then owned the course – invited Prince Edward (later King Edward VII) to become its President. In turn, the current Queen became patron in 1952, holding the position for over 50 years, until she handed over to Prince Charles in 2002.

The track is left-handed and square-looking and, since it is only 1 mile in extent, is a tight affair that is less well-suited to long-striding gallopers than to handy front-running types that can cope well with its none-too-severe undulations.

The 200-yard uphill run-in is the only course feature that is in any way testing, since Fakenham's six fences are far from formidable and good ground is much more common than firm, soft or heavy going, such is the excellent drainage provided by the course's sandy subsoil.

In 2001, Fakenham saw the construction of a new members grandstand with panoramic views of the course and a 40-seat restaurant. The course's facilities are likely to see a further major upgrade as it has secured European funding for an additional grandstand with public and private entertaining rooms.

Rail travellers will find, rather irritatingly, that after travelling from London King's Cross or Liverpool Street to King's Lynn or Norwich, they will still have a journey of some 22 miles to complete to reach the course, which is more conveniently accessible from the former town on the A148 than from the latter on the A1067. Some local bus services do, however, service the course from the rail station. Air travellers in fixed-winged aircraft may land at Little Snoring airstrip which is five miles from the course.

FAKENHAM: Plan of the course. Its proximity to the royal residence of Sandringham is one of the reasons why this small East Anglian course plays host to the Queen's Cup and the Prince of Wales' Cup.

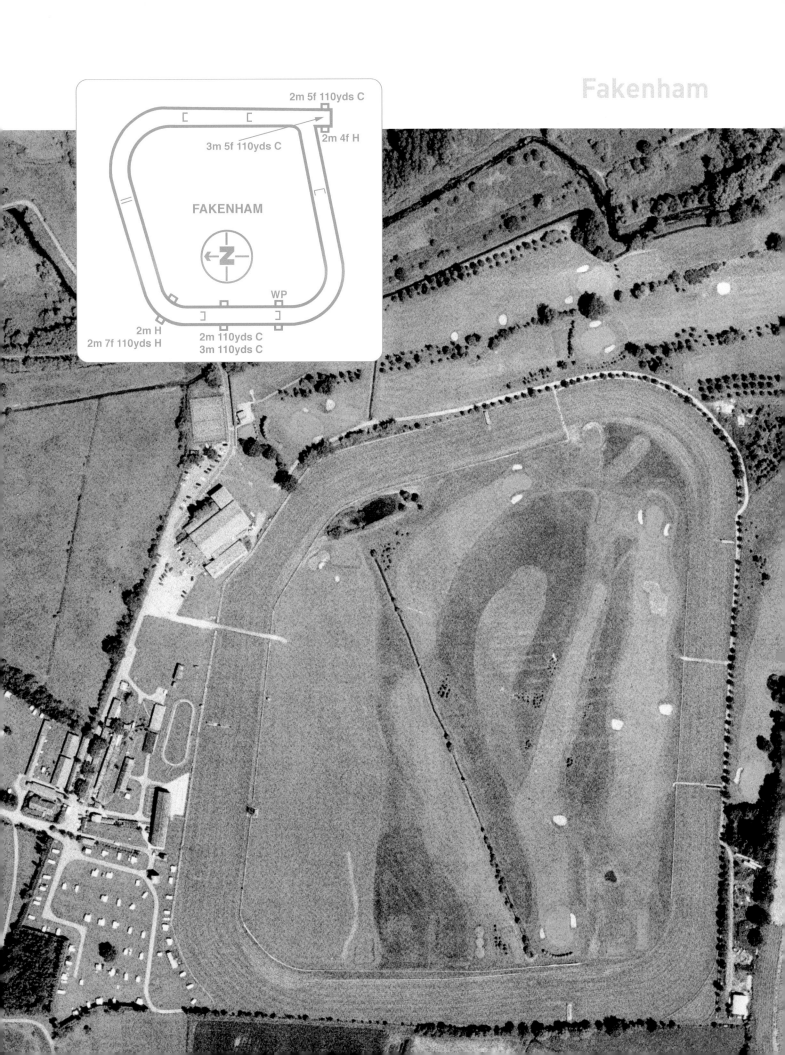

Fakenham

2m 5f 110yds C

2m 4f H

3m 5f 110yds C

FAKENHAM

WP

2m H
2m 7f 110yds H

2m 110yds C
3m 110yds C

Folkestone

Folkestone Racecourse
Westenhanger
Hythe
Kent CT21 4HX
Tel 0870 220 0023
www.folkestone-racecourse.co.uk

HOW TO GET THERE:
From North: B2068 (from Canterbury)
From South: A259 (from Hastings)
From East: M20 (Junct. 11)
From West: M20 (Junct. 11)
By Rail: Westenhanger
By Air: Helicopter facilities

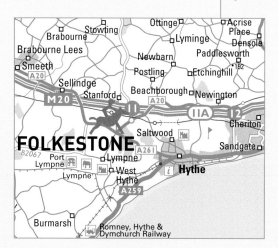

Just to the north of Hythe, seven miles north-east of Folkestone, is the only track now left in the 'Garden of England'. It occupies a suitably pretty site at Westenhanger adjoining a country station of that name which lies on the main lines to the Kent coast from Charing Cross or Victoria, approximately 70 miles away. Londoners travelling here by road should take the A20 and then leave the M20 at junction 11.

The track itself is a pear-shaped affair that runs right-handed for 1 mile and 3 furlongs over ground that, although it frequently undulates, does so in none-too-pronounced a fashion.

Horses contesting races over 2 miles 93 yards, 1 mile 7 furlongs 92 yards and 1½ miles start from various points along the 6-furlong course, past the stands, and then make a complete circuit of the round course, before finally negotiating the run-in of approximately 3 furlongs.

The 6-furlong course, which is straight throughout, features some gently undulating terrain and includes a slight rise near its end.

When the stalls are positioned on the stands side, high-drawn runners are slightly favoured at Folkestone in 5- and 6-furlong sprints. Similarly, in races run on the fairly tight right-handed turns of the round course, the advantage lies with those allotted high positions in the stalls, especially in races over 1 mile 1 furlong 149 yards and 12 furlongs since these particular distances involve so much turning track.

'Handy' horses which are adaptable and sure-footed, tend to appreciate Folkestone's fairly sharp and awkwardly right-handed bends and its frequent undulations that make it resemble a rather gentle switchback. Runners on both the straight and the round courses need to be ridden by experienced jockeys who can keep them balanced if the ground becomes slippery.

Folkestone is generally considered to be an easy course that does not really favour the long-striding, resolute galloper whose strong suit is stamina. Indeed, short runners, if handled by tactically astute jockeys, can win over distances on this rather lowly track over which they would not triumph elsewhere.

The 1962 2000 Guineas winner Privy Councillor has been commemorated by a prestigious flat race (a 6-furlong sprint for three-year-olds). The 5-furlong Folkestone Stakes for three-year-olds is staged at the end of May.

National Hunt racing is also staged at Westenhanger

over eight very easy obstacles and the fact that the run-in for steeplechasers only extends for a furlong (and that for hurdlers for only an additional 30 yards) means that nippy front-running jumpers often enjoy an advantage.

One particular evening meeting in May is confined to hunter 'chasers and attracts both followers of hounds and point-to-point. Its light-hearted atmosphere seems appropriate, as one race staged is the Cuckoo Novices' Hunter Chase.

Folkestone's French connection, much strengthened by the building of the Channel Tunnel, has been recalled by such races as the Le Touquet Novices Hurdle.

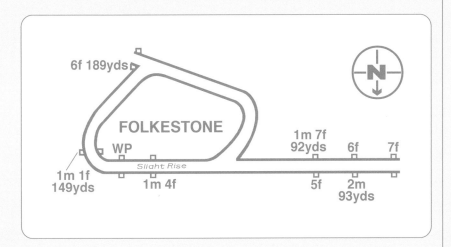

FOLKESTONE: Plan of the Flat course (left), and the National Hunt course (bottom).

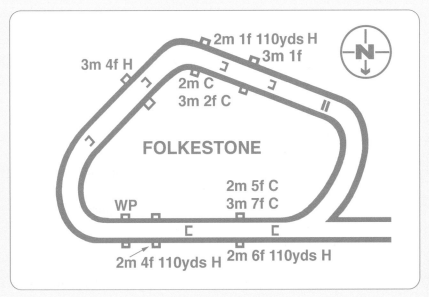

[072] Folkestone

Fontwell Park

Figure-of-eight courses leave some horses at sixes and sevens and that is why those that have repeatedly shown that they relish running on its left-and-right-handed 'chase course are often worth yet another interest at Fontwell Park. The situation and picturesque setting of this singular Sussex course that lies between Goodwood and Chichester less than 60 miles from London explain its popularity. Most Londoners arrive at the track initially via the M23 and then take the A29 until it meets the A27. Thereafter, the course is well signposted.

Rail travellers should head for Barnham station, which is readily accessible from Victoria, and then take a three-mile bus ride to the course which offers no facilities for air travellers.

A good view is available from the three grandstands of the somewhat disorientating sight of steeplechasers negotiating the fences on Fontwell's tight track of just over a mile. This ends with a short run-in of only 230 yards which, rather distinctively, runs uphill and slightly to the left and so makes a last further demand on the adaptability of the 'chasers that have finally to tackle it.

Nickel Coin, the 1951 Grand National winner, is recalled by a 'chase run at Fontwell over 2½ miles. This race is staged at an autumn meeting.

As for hurdlers, the well-known 1966 Champion Hurdler Salmon Spray has been commemorated by a Fontwell contest staged in late October. This, like all 2 mile 2 furlong races run over the minor obstacles on this track, only involves tight left-handed turns and nine flights in all.

Fontwell Park Racecourse
Fontwell
Near Arundel
West Sussex BN18 0SX
Tel: (01243) 543335
www.fontwellpark.co.uk

HOW TO GET THERE:
From North: A29 (from Billingshurst)
From South: A29 (from Bognor Regis)
From East: A27 (from Brighton)
From West: A27 (from Chichester)
By Rail: Barnham (free coach to course)
By Air: Chichester Aerodrome

FONTWELL PARK: Plan of the course.

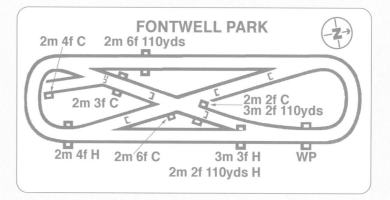

Galway

Fairly riotous celebration has always been something of a feature at Galway ever since a band of hard-riding sportsmen from the local hunt acquired their rather apt name of the Blazers by burning down a nearby hotel. Indeed, the hospitality at Galway's legendary week-long festival meeting in late July and early August is so overpowering that one needs as much stamina as the horses to last the course.

In quieter moments one can appreciate the view of Galway castle and the beautiful backdrop provided by the far-off Clare coastline.

Galway's right-handed track might appear to be a fairly easy affair but is anything but that, as an uphill run to the last jump is cunningly contrived to find out the non-stayer. The course, a distinct switchback only about 1 mile 2 furlongs round, is a tight, sharp affair over which past winners naturally have a good record; some judges believe high-drawn horses have a slight advantage in races run over 7 furlongs and 1 mile.

The popular Galway Plate regularly attracts the attention of English trainers and jockeys. Other well-known festival races that have proved popular have been the G.P.T. Qualified Riders Handicap, the Guinness Galway Hurdle and the McDonogh E.B.F. Handicap. A 'Best Dressed Lady Competition' is also a festival feature.

The autumn meeting generally involves three days in early September. Here one of the most prestigious races contested is the Carl Scarpa Handicap Hurdle (in which it is perhaps unwise to invest with bookmakers seen hammering spikes into their shoes), while a potent 'chaser' to the Oyster Stakes is provided by the Smirnoff Handicap Chase.

Some racegoers travel to the track daily on the N59 from accommodation taken on the Connemara coast. The many 'Dubs' who drive in from their country's capital do so along the N4 and N6, while Limerick-based racegoers can travel north on the N18. Galway station is well served.

To many Irish racegoers Galway is the National Hunt season. It certainly is a meeting at which the volume of money wagered is prodigious and the 'craic' unrivalled.

Galway races, it seems, date back to the eighteenth century and in the words of Arthur Macgahon 'still live up to those exciting days when a horseman in a hunt or race who did not choose the highest stone wall or jump the most dangerous course to follow, was a man who would never do for Galway'!

Galway Racecourse
Ballybrit
Galway
Ireland
Tel: +353 (0)91 753870
www.galwayraces.com

HOW TO GET THERE:
From North: N17; N84
From South: N18
From East: N6
From West: N59; R336
By Rail: Galway
By Air: Galway Carnmore Airport

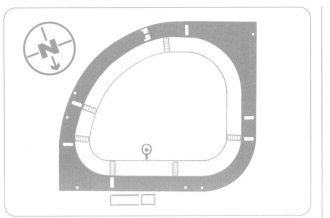

GALWAY: Plan of the course

Goodwood

Goodwood Racecourse
Goodwood
Chichester
West Sussex, PO18 0PS
Tel: (01243) 755022
www.gloriousgoodwood.co.uk

HOW TO GET THERE:
From North: A3; A286
From South: A259 (from Bognor Regis)
From East: A27 (from Lewes); A285
From West: A27 (from Havant); A286 (from Chichester)
By Rail: Victoria or Waterloo to Chichester (5 miles); bus/taxi to course
By Air: Goodwood Aerodrome; Helicopter facilities (2 miles)

Goodwood, like Epsom and Royal Ascot, is not just a racecourse, but also the setting for a social occasion of some significance. The track is one of the most peculiarly shaped and picturesque in the world.

That the course should be so distinctive was the deliberate intention of the two men responsible for its creation and development, the Duke of Richmond and Lord George Bentinck. As a typical Victorian patrician, the former was anxious that racing be 'divested of its coarse and disgusting accessories'. Since his extensive private estate took in a crest of the Sussex Downs, he had an ideal opportunity both to create a distinctive racecourse and to deny entrance to undesirables.

Thus, almost from its inception, Goodwood became part of the social season. Still today, many of those who go racing to be seen will be found at Goodwood's main midsummer festival.

It seems appropriate that currently the most expensive enclosure, from which in Victorian times even the divorced were excluded, is now known as the 'Richmond', after the fastidious aristocrat.

The Duke would doubtless have been disconcerted had he lived until 1875 to witness the Bohemian behaviour then seen on Trundle Hill, now a cheap rather than a free enclosure well beyond the pale, whose patrons pay a modest sum for a rather distant view of the racing.

It seems unfair that, while the Duke is commemorated through the 6-furlong Richmond Stakes run at the main midsummer festival meeting, Lord George Bentinck, who may have hastened his early death by so energetically designing and laying out the present track, is recalled only by a race that is named after Surplice, the horse he sold two years before its Derby triumph in 1848.

The singular course, which has hardly changed since Bentinck's day, is a complex affair whose peculiarities conspire to produce one of the most breathtaking sights in British racing.

Basically it resembles an equilateral triangle that has lost one of its sides. The far side is very unusual in that it features a tight loop and two turns for home. Horses racing over 5 furlongs encounter one of the fastest sprint courses in Britain and start from stalls that are positioned only a few yards beyond the point at which horses taking part in 7- and 8-furlong events round the lower of the home turns. The best known 5-furlong sprints staged at Goodwood are the King George Stakes, in which three-

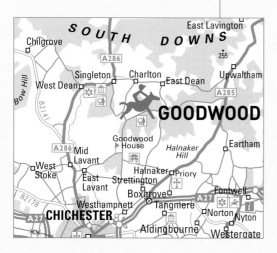

year-olds often go well, and the Molecomb Stakes for first-season performers.

A spur which extends beyond the 5-furlong gate allows exciting 6-furlong events to be staged on a straight course known as the 'Stewards' Cup' course, after an historic and highly competitive handicap and heavy betting medium that is quite often won by a three-year-old that can fly along this far from level course. Right from the start, the horses face a taxing climb for a furlong or so and then encounter ground that falls sharply. Thereafter, they have less of a switchback to negotiate.

Horses taking part in Goodwood sprints enjoy an advantage if they can fly from the gate or are habitual front runners. So much descending ground will further suit types ridden by experienced jockeys who can both keep them balanced and help them conserve something for the closing stages of their 'cavalry charge'.

Several important races over the less common distance of 7 furlongs are contested at Goodwood.

Horses that run over 7 or 8 furlongs on this track run round the lower and the sharper of the two bends into the straight and then face what is an unusually long run-in of almost 5 furlongs. Success in these races often goes to horses well rated by stop-watch holders that can take undulating ground in their stride and handle what must be one of the sharpest, if well-banked, right-handed bends in the country.

Of pattern races run over a mile, the Sussex Stakes staged in midsummer is regarded by many as the 'Mile Championship of Europe'. Three-year-olds often run in both this and the 1-mile Celebration Mile that is contested a month or so later.

Just under ten-furlong events are staged over what has been called the 'Craven' course, which starts on the near side of the loop. From here, the runners make their way home by the shortest route which takes them round the higher and more gradual of the bends into the finishing straight. This track is used to stage the Predominate Stakes, the well-known Lupe Stakes in May and the even more prestigious Nassau Stakes for fillies and mares.

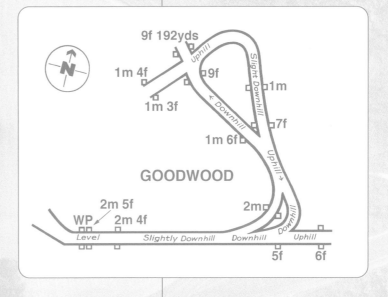

GOODWOOD: Plan of the course.

Another near mile-and-a-quarter race, the Select Stakes, is a weight for age contest staged in September, in which it often pays to side with a four-year-old.

Races over a full 12 furlongs are run over what was once known as the 'Gratwicke' course. This severe test of stamina starts from a short spur which extends from the top of the loop on its near side. Its first furlong is straight, but after running uphill it swings to the right, quite gradually at first and then very sharply as it rounds the north-eastern side of the clump, a raised section of the course that lies within the loop.

From this point, the runners enter the straight on the far side of the loop and drop down into an appreciable dip that makes them temporarily invisible to grandstand patrons. A downhill run into the finishing straight via the lower of the two home turns completes the course. The most important 12-furlong race staged each year is the Gordon Stakes for three-year-olds whose running often provides a St Leger pointer.

Events over 1¾ miles are run over what is known as the 'Bentinck' course, which appropriately takes in almost all of the track designed by Lord George.

Long-distance races provide Goodwood racegoers with much prolonged pleasure and some are run over 2 miles and 4 furlongs in front of the grandstands some way down the finishing straight. After negotiating this part of the track over which they race in reverse, the runners negotiate a left-hand bend that turns quite sharply into a straight section of less than a furlong. After this, the track describes something of a dog leg as it diverges slightly to the left on its way to the 1¾-mile start and the loop at the top of the course.

Until recently the 2 mile 5 furlong course presented runners in an historic race, the Goodwood Cup, with an even more demanding test of stamina and adaptability – only at Ascot and Pontefract are longer distances raced over on the flat in Britain. This was once known as the 'Cup' course after the time-honoured Goodwood Cup, first staged as long ago as 1812, the year of Napoleon's retreat from Moscow! Interestingly, this particular race provided the French with a victory of a very different type when Beggarman triumphed in its 1840 running and thus recorded one of the earliest Gallic triumphs on the British turf.

By tradition, horses taking part in this particular marathon lined up for a flag start and jumped off from a point well under a furlong beyond the winning post. After they raced the 'wrong' way along the

home straight, they faced exactly the same taxing experience as horses do in the 'new' Goodwood Cup now run over over 2 miles. In the past many previous winners of the then slightly shorter Ascot Gold Cup went on to take the Goodwood Cup, but the now reduced (2 mile) distance of this race threatens this possibility.

Many races on this course make considerable demands on a horse's stamina if they are run at speed over its severely undulating sections. However, it is sometimes possible for an experienced jockey to win on a doubtful stayer. This is because the many turns and banks on this track make it possible for such a rider to position his horse so that it is prevented from perceiving clearly what lies ahead of it. Such a tactic can be tantamount to removing as much as 7 lbs from its back. Gordon Richards was apparently most adept in covering up many of his Goodwood mounts in this way so that they could become neither bored nor daunted. In fact, many a long-striding dour stayer finds it difficult to cope with the sharp turns and steep descents of the round course and thus can be beaten by a horse covered up in the Richards style.

THE GRANDSTAND: Goodwood, like Epsom Downs and Royal Ascot is not just a racecourse, but also the setting for a social occasion of some significance – the track is one of the most peculiarly shaped and picturesque in the world.

Goodwood

The going at Goodwood is seldom heavy since a porous chalky subsoil lies beneath its lush downland turf. In the rather rare event of soft going, some jockeys tend to move their mounts over to the stands side where the ground is supposed to be easier to negotiate.

As for the draw on this delightfully picturesque course, those allotted high stalls positions in races from 7 to 12 furlongs seem to be favoured.

Firm going is a distinct possibility at Goodwood, since four of its meetings take place in late summer or the autumn, yet the turf is sufficiently springy to take the jar out of the ground.

The view at Goodwood, especially from the main grandstand, is regarded by many as the finest on a British racecourse and thus it is perhaps appropriate that a race is staged annually in memory of the BBC racing commentator, Clive Graham. The course is 706 feet above sea level, providing an excellent vantage point from which to view the Sussex Downs and the distant English Channel. For these and several other reasons, 'glorious' Goodwood marks, for many racegoers, the highlight of the flat racing season.

Hamilton Park

Racing at Hamilton, which is pleasantly situated 10 miles south-east of Glasgow, first took place in July 1888 when the dream of a group of whisky distillers, of bringing horseracing nearer to Glasgow, finally came to fruition in a fenced-off section of a park belonging to Lord Hamilton. The present track has been raced on since July 1926 and it was the venue for Britain's first-ever evening meeting in July 1947.

Glasgow Airport should figure in the flight plan of air travellers, while those arriving by rail, perhaps from London Euston, should travel on from Glasgow Central to Hamilton West station.

Motorists making the short trip from Glasgow should leave the M74 at junction 5 (those coming from England and the south should leave at junction 6). Then, like those driving in from Edinburgh (who should leave the M8 at junction 6), they should look for signs indicating the B7071 along which the course will be found between Hamilton and Bothwell. The proximity of a local mausoleum should not deter racegoers!

The Hamilton Park course is a compact, peculiarly shaped 13-furlong affair, rather reminiscent of a badminton racquet complete with a carrying strap at the end of its handle! Its straight course consists of a 6 furlong 5 yard stretch.

Horses in the sprints face a fairly stiff task, since the surface they race over is far from level, the undulations on the 5 furlong 4 yard and 6 furlong 5 yard courses being reminiscent of a switchback. Horses racing on the latter track start from a short spur and initially race over fairly level ground. Subsequently, this descends (quite gently at first, then steeply) into a dip near the 3-furlong pole. This infamous feature has effectively 'found out' many well-fancied and handily placed contestants. Thanks to the spending of over £100,000 to improve drainage and ground consistency, heavy going is now seldom encountered at Hamilton.

In the closing stages of Hamilton sprints, the contestants face another rather punishing test of their strength. After emerging from the dip, they have to negotiate ground that rises gradually at first and then much more steeply in the penultimate furlong. Indeed, respite only comes in the closing stages when level ground is finally encountered.

Highly drawn sprinters seem to be favoured at Hamilton (when, especially on soft or heavy ground, the stalls are placed on the stands side) as are horses which contest races over 1 mile 65 yards and 9 furlongs 36 yards since,

Hamilton Park Racecourse
Bothwell Road
Hamilton
Lanarkshire ML3 0DW
Tel: (01698) 283806
www.hamilton-park.co.uk

HOW TO GET THERE:
From North: M9 (Junct. 9); M80 (Junct. 4); A80
From South: M74 (Junct. 6)
From East: M8 (Junct. 6)
From West: A8; M8; M74 (Junct. 5)
By Rail: Hamilton West
By Air: Glasgow Airport

they have to run round a semi-circular section of track that bends appreciably to the right before it joins the straight course shortly before the 5-furlong gate.

Horses taking part in races over 11 furlongs 16 yards and 12 furlongs 17 yards actually jump off from points along the straight that are even nearer the winning post, and they are then ridden the 'wrong' way down the course.

Long-distance events over 1 mile 5 furlongs 9 yards are also run 'in reverse' and are started from a point just beyond the winning post, which means that those involved have a rather rare initial opportunity to race over a level stretch of ground!

The sweeping right-handed turns at Hamilton are fairly gentle and thus make no great demands on jockeyship which, however, is tested to the full by several other features of this track. If horses perform best when 'held up' they may well appreciate the long 5-furlong run-in on which it is possible for an experienced jockey to ride a late finish to good effect.

In recent seasons the Hamilton executive hase devised several schemes and improved facilities to attract not only Glaswegians, but racegoers from all over the central belt of Scotland. Hamilton stages eight evening meetings which include a Saints and Sinners event, a Velvet Fair Friday and a Ladies' Night. A hugely popular five-star package is also on offer to racegoers. These attractions and a recent 52 per cent increase in annual prize money augur well for Hamilton's future.

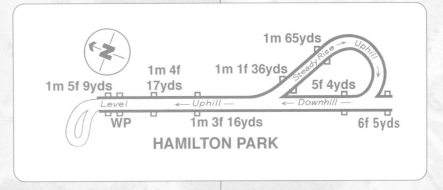

HAMILTON PARK: Plan of the course.

Hamilton Park

Haydock Park

Haydock Park Racecourse
Newton-le-Willows
Merseyside WA12 0HQ
Tel: (01942) 725963
www.haydock-park.co.uk

HOW TO GET THERE:
From North: M6 (Junct. 23); M61 (Junct. 1); A580
From South: M6 (Junct. 23)
From East: M62 (Junct. 15); A580
From West: A580 (from Bootle)
By Rail: Newton-le-Willows (Manchester–Liverpool line or Warrington Bank Quay, London (Euston)–Glasgow line)
By Air: Helicopter facilities; course airstrip

Haydock Park racecourse came into being at the close of the nineteenth century. Its recent development and support by the Levy Board, its status as the north-west's premier racecourse, its proximity to the M6 and M61 motorways and the vast population centres of Manchester and Liverpool, as well as its excellent facilities, all account for its popularity.

Some London-based racegoers start their 200-mile journey to the track by taking a train from Euston to Wigan or Warrington Bank Quay (mainline) and thereafter find that a taxi-ride is necessary. The alternative is to motor to junction 23 of the M6 and then follow the signs directing patrons a further half-mile or so to the course, which lies on the A49 near Ashton.

Haydock offers its patrons such facilities as a new members' stand, refurbished Tattersalls areas, a brand new parade ring and paddock under the famous Haydock Park trees, and a clear view of its high-class racing. The 13-furlong circuit itself is oval and virtually flat.

Haydock's left-hand bends are fairly easy to negotiate and its many extensive straight sections – two of which form a kink or elbow in its back stretch – allow long-striding, galloping types to come into their own.

Negotiation of the long 4-furlong or so straight run-in, which rises slightly but almost continuously for much of its length, makes a final demand on the stamina of all those that run on this important top-class track. It is also an experience that is appreciated by horses that have to be 'held up' and prevented from making a premature finishing effort.

Those tackling sprint distances at Haydock enjoy a double advantage if they are fast starters and, if the stalls are positioned on the stands side, they are highly drawn on what is a straight section of track. When the going is soft this particular advantage is increased, particularly over 6 furlongs, over which, in early September the Group One Sprint Cup is staged, a race that is frequently captured by a four-year-old.

When the ground is dry, horses allocated low numbers in the draw are favoured in races over 7 furlongs 30 yards, since for a fair proportion of this particular distance, they negotiate a semi-circular, if fairly gentle, left-hand bend. The best-known race run over this unusual race distance is the listed John of Gaunt Stakes that is contested on Derby day.

'Mile' races at Haydock, such as the important Tote Silver Bowl staged in late May, actually involve a distance of 1 mile 30 yards and start from a point along one of the two straight sections of track on the back straight.

The Rose of Lancaster Group Three Race over 10 furlongs 120 yards involves the kink in the course about 9 furlongs out, while horses that tackle a further furlong and 80 yards run over a course on which the prestigious Lancashire Oaks for three-year-old fillies is run in late June or early July – this latter race being on the same main card as the Old Newton Cup Handicap, which is named after the original racecourse a short distance away from the current location.

Long-distance races over 2 miles 45 yards are also staged at Haydock and are started from a point in the finishing straight that lies between the 4- and the 3-furlong poles.

With its ten testingly stiff obstacles, many of them drop fences, Haydock is a jumping track on which a victory for a chaser augurs well for a run over the Grand National obstacles at Liverpool.

The course holds a number of important jumping meetings that attract the best steeplechasers the north has to offer. In January the main pre-Cheltenham meeting takes place and includes three prestigious races: a Champion Hurdle trial, a Long Distance Hurdle of 23½ furlongs and the Peter Marsh Chase over 3 miles. An important Grand National prep race, the well-established Haydock Park Gold Cup in which seven- and nine-year-olds seem to go well, is also staged some weeks before the Cheltenham Festival at a late February/early March Haydock fixture. This 3 mile 4½ furlong 'chase is staged on the same day as the final of Haydock Park's 'brush hurdle' series. This extremely successful series is run over 'French-style' obstacles (mini-fences), and has been a great boost for trainers bringing through their future chasers.

HAYDOCK PARK: Plans of the Flat course (top) and the National Hunt course (bottom).

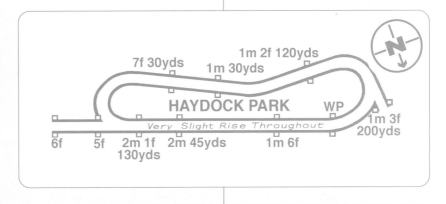

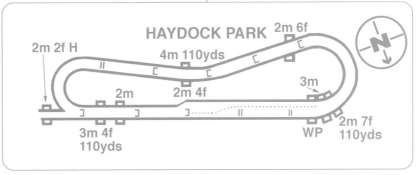

Haydock Park

Before Christmas, Haydock's other major staying chases are run – the Edward Hanmer Chase in November and Tommy Whittle Chase in December – both Grade Two, 3-mile chases which always attract some of the country's leading jumpers.

All steeplechasers at Haydock have to negotiate a water jump positioned in front of the stands. This obstacle and the open ditch are not jumped on the final circuit which ends in a run-in of around 2 furlongs.

Hurdle races at Haydock are staged on a rather tight track that runs inside the 'chasing circuit, and again there is a long run-in which often sees the lead change hands.

Hereford

This right-handed track of 12 furlongs is a mile away from the railway station of the county town whose name it bears (itself 123 miles from London Paddington) . It can be reached by heading north out of Hereford on the A49, is the road that should be used by racegoers travelling south from Ludlow and Leominster. The A49 and then the A495 are recommended to southern-based visitors, while those from the Midlands may arrive from Worcester.

The course (now into its fourth century) lies in a pleasantly rural location that also contains a golf course.

Hereford provides a searching test of the jumpers it attracts in fairly large numbers since they have to race the 'wrong' (right-handed) way round it, cope with nine fairly stiff obstacles and tackle a sharp downhill home turn. These particular course features make it worthwhile to consider past course and distance winners, especially those sent out by handlers whose runners have achieved excellent wins to runs ratios.

Hereford's appeal perhaps explains why Sir Piers Bengough, formerly Her Majesty the Queen's representative at Ascot, has officiated as a steward at its fixtures, at one of which, a hurdle race is staged in memory of Fred Rimell, the famous jockey and trainer from nearby Worcestershire.

Hereford Racecourse
Roman Road
Holmer
Hereford HR4 9QU
Tel: (01432) 273560
www.hereford-racecourse.co.uk

HOW TO GET THERE:
From North: A49 (from Ludlow and Leominster)
From South: A49 (from Ross-on-Wye)
From East: A438 (from Ledbury)
From West: A40; A438 (from Brecon)
By Rail: Hereford
By Air: Helicopter facilities

HEREFORD: Plan of the course. Racing here is staged in a clockwise direction.

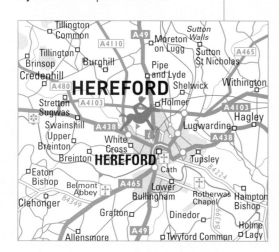

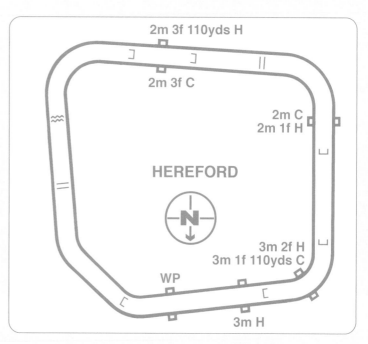

Hexham

Hexham can rival some scenically impressive Irish country courses, such is the splendour of its rural location. A hillside 800 feet above sea level provides the ideal site for its grandstand from which a magnificent view can be gained of steeplechasers taking its ten fences. These, despite being easy, are positioned on a 12-furlong, left-handed track that is testing in nature as its later stages include a steep climb, respite from which is only offered by a short 250-yard run-in that eventually features flat ground.

Another configurational peculiarity is a downhill stretch that extends (from the point where races over 2 miles 4 1/2 furlongs are started) for almost half a mile to a pronounced dip. Not surprisingly, on this taxing track one should side with runners with proven stamina and which are adaptable enough to cope with its quite severe gradients.

Hexham Racecourse
High Yarridge
Hexham
Northumberland NE46 2JP
Tel: (01434) 606881
Caterers (dining room): Ramside
0191 236 4148
www.hexham-racecourse.co.uk

HOW TO GET THERE:
From North: A68; A69
From South: A68; A69
From East: A69 (from Newcastle upon Tyne)
From West: A69 (from Brampton)
By Rail: Hexham (free bus from station)
By Air: Helicopter facilities; Newcastle upon Tyne airport

Since Hexham is 280 miles from London, some southerners are deterred from attending its fixtures although these are savoured by many of racing's cognoscenti. The point-to-point, rather Corinthian flavour of this Northumberland gaff is only to be expected since the principal race it stages is the fine-sounding Heart of All England Hunters' Steeplechase.

Air travellers will need to leave their (fixed-wing) aircraft at Newcastle upon Tyne's airport, while those travelling from London King's Cross will find Hexham station is a 1½-mile bus or taxi-ride from the course. Motorists should head for the A69 which links Carlisle with Newcastle and will find the course lying 38 miles east of the former town and 20 miles west of the latter.

Racegoers should note that Hexham's exposed situation is such that no fixtures are held in February. Much has been done to improve the comfort for racegoers over the past ten years. The latest addition is a 70-seater dining room for which booking is essential on Saturdays.

Winners at Hexham often perform well at lowlier and less-taxing Sedgefield.

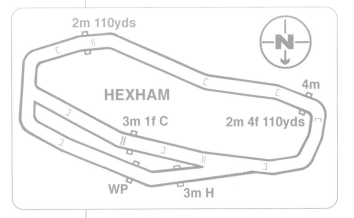

Huntingdon

Despite being far from scenically splendid, Huntingdon has a convenient location just off the A1 and the excellent drainage provided by its gravel subsoil means its fixtures are seldom rained off.

Like much of East Anglia, this track is flat and fairly featureless; a right-handed oval that extends for 12 furlongs. There are nine fences on its circuit which ends in a shortish run-in of only 200 yards.

Horses well-rated by stop-watch holders go well on this track which can be taken at speed by runners able to handle itsright-handed configuration. For this reason, past course and distance winners that are top-rated on time are worth consideration. A few horses, particularly novices, are troubled by the track's penultimate fence, but this, and another in the finishing straight, are the only two difficult obstacles.

The course lies 21 miles north-east of Bedford, just outside Brampton, itself 2½ miles from Huntingdon, so Londoners have only 60 miles to motor to the track. Rail travellers when alighting at Huntingdon (a stop on the express route from Edinburgh to London King's Cross) will find they have a further 2½ miles to travel to the course by taxi. There is a fixed-wing aircraft landing strip a mile from the course and helicopters have landed in its centre by prior arrangement.

Huntingdon Racecourse
Brampton
Huntingdon
Cambridgeshire PE28 4NL
Tel: (01480) 453373
www.huntingdon-racecourse.co.uk

HOW TO GET THERE:
From North: A1(M); A141 (from Wisbech)
From South: A1 (from Letchworth)
From East: A14 (from Cambridge, Newmarket)
From West: A14 (from Kettering)
By Rail: Huntingdon
By Air: Helicopter facilities

HUNTINGDON: Plan of the course.

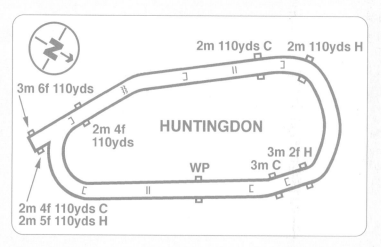

Kelso

Kelso Racecourse
Kelso
Roxburghshire
Scotland TD5 7SX
Tel: (01573) 224767
www.kelso-races.co.u

Racecourse office:
18–20 Glendale Road
Wooler, Northumberland NE71 6DW
Tel: (01668) 280800

HOW TO GET THERE:
From North: (from Edinburgh)
A68; A697; A6089
From South: M6 (Junct. 44); A7; A698
From East: (from Berwick-upon-Tweed) A698
From West: (from Falkirk) A699
By Rail: Berwick-upon-Tweed (22 miles)
By Air: Helicopter facilities; Edinburgh Airport

Berwick-upon-Tweed is the nearest railway station to this gem of a 'gaff' which is over 300 miles from London King's Cross. The journey is extended by a rather expensive 22-mile taxi-ride to the course itself.

Understandably then, most racegoers journeying from the south arrive by car via the M6 to junction 44, before taking the A7 and A698 to Kelso, or the B6364; the course, which is in aristocratic ownership, lies only half a mile to the north of this pleasantly situated border town. Southerners daunted by the thought of driving all the way to Kelso and back on a winter's day can fly in for the races, either in helicopters that can land on the course by prior arrangement or in fixed-wing aircraft that can be accommodated at Winfield Duns, a 15-mile taxi-drive away. Alternatively, they can disembark at Edinburgh International Airport, an hour's drive away.

Kelso consists of two sharp, left-handed courses. The circuit that 'chasers have to negotiate extends for 1 mile 600 yards and the even tighter hurdle track for only 1 mile 330 yards. Clearly then, long-striding types are at a disadvantage. However, the bends at Kelso have been levelled out lately and the 'chase course, especially, is now much more galloping. Nevertheless, 'chasers that lack courage and resolution may not be suited to Kelso since, after negotiating a downhill back stretch of track that contains tricky fences, they face a far from straight and quite punishing uphill run-in of 2 furlongs.

Good going, good visibility and very good cheer can almost be guaranteed at Kelso whose principal races are all 'chases. That one has been the King's Own Challenge Cup seems highly appropriate since this is 'Scottish soldier' country, not far from the town of Coldstream. The fact that so many of its fixtures involve rather short winter days (that thankfully are generally free of fog) might explain the strange rule that on-course picnics are not allowed at Kelso!

Kelso

2m 1f C
3m 4f C
2m 110yds H
3m 3f H

HURDLE COURSE

KELSO

2m 2f H

2m 6f 110yds H

2m 4f 110yds H

WP

3m 1f C

2m 6f 110yds C

4m C

KELSO: Plan of the course.

Kempton Park

Kempton Park Racecourse
Staines Road
Sunbury-on-Thames
Middlesex TW16 5AQ
Tel: (01932) 782292
www.kempton.co.uk

HOW TO GET THERE:
From North: M1 (Junct. 6A); M25 (Junct. 13); A308
From South: A3; M25; M3 (Junct. 1)
From East: M20 (Junct. 3); M26; M25 (Junct. 12)
From West: A303; M3 (Junct. 1)
By Rail: Kempton Park
By Air: Helicopter facilities

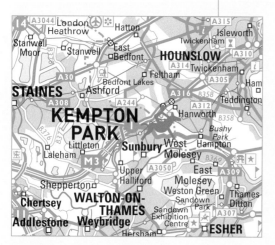

It was once the custom to hold British race meetings on common land and thus to throw them open to all comers.

In 1878, those responsible for building Kempton Park did much to pioneer and popularize the novel concept of charging admission to fully enclosed courses. The 300-acre site on which they chose to construct this suburban course near Sunbury-on-Thames, 16 miles south-west of London, had once been parkland of sufficient importance to be mentioned in Domesday Book.

This popular course is only half a mile away from the first exit of the M3 and, as London's most accessible course, has its own racecourse railway station that can be reached from Waterloo. Motorists heading for Sunbury from the capital are advised to approach on the A316 to the M3, while those travelling from the west should also take this particular motorway, before finally driving half a mile to the track along the A308.

A glance through old racing annuals confirms the sad fact that Kempton was once a much more prestigious venue for flat racing than has been the case in recent decades. The particular race for which Kempton was long best known – the Jubilee Handicap Stakes – was once an important spring handicap. Today it is simply a fairly important mile handicap that, although it is the highlight of Kempton's early May meeting, is a rather pale reflection of its former self.

The course itself, which Fred Archer once rather intriguingly described as a 'sirloin of beef cut the wrong way' has a circumference of 1 mile 5 furlongs. It is an almost perfectly flat, right-angled triangle that is bisected diagonally by yet another separate course that cuts across its longest side. This is a dead straight sprint track on which events over 5 and 6 furlongs are staged under circumstances that favour high-drawn runners if the stalls are placed on the far side. If, however, the ground is soft, the opposite may apply.

The spur that helps to provide the sprint course is much longer than the rather stubby affair that projects from the penultimate bend on the round course and thus allows races to be staged over 9 furlongs.

Yet another long straight spur that projects from the final bend allows 10-, 8- and 7-furlong events to take place at Kempton Park. Since the Jubilee Handicap was (from 1887 to 1978) staged over its full extent, rather than over a mile as at present, this right-hand dog leg is known as the 'Jubilee' course, on which the effect of the draw can be discounted.

Instead of running their miles over the extensive straight section of the 'Jubilee' course, trainers can let them take their chances on the 'round' course on which events over 11 furlongs 30 yards, as well as 12, 14 furlongs 92 yards and 16 furlongs are also staged.

Currently, the Queen's Prize, a handicap run over 2 miles at Kempton's important Easter meeting, once sufficiently important to be classed as a particularly prestigious spring handicap, does not even qualify for 'listed' status.

Runners tackling 2-mile races need both stamina and, above all, speed if they are to triumph on the round course which, being fairly tight, tends to favour small, neat, handy types that can adapt readily to running so much of their races the 'wrong' way round. Such stayers have to negotiate three fairly sweeping right-handed turns that make up Kempton's triangular circuit.

A premium is placed on jockeyship if, rather unusually, the Kempton going is soft. If this is the case, the best ground lies either in the centre of the track or near the stands' rails and can be best approached if jockeys swing wide as they take the final turn into the 3½-furlong run-in. Kempton also stages the Easter Stakes at its two-day spring meeting, as well as the Masaka Stakes.

Kempton's Group races are the Sirenia Stakes, a 6 furlong juvenile event and the September Stakes, run over 11 furlongs 30 yards. Both take place about a week before the St Leger.

In recent seasons, Kempton's rather splendid jumping fixtures

KEMPTON PARK: Plans of the Flat course (top) and the National Hunt course (bottom).

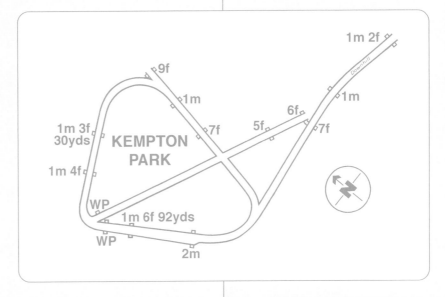

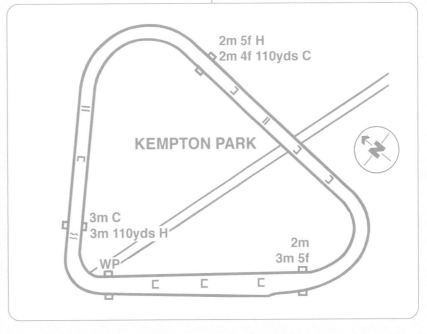

Kempton Park

have attracted far more racegoers than its flat-race programmes. The best-known race – and not just for being farmed by Desert Orchid – is the King George VI Chase, the event that above all others the racing enthusiast associates with Christmas. This 3-mile Boxing Day spectacular that, in its most recent past, has often given the same French trainer a joyeux Noël, is notable for the amazing number of repeat victories its results have featured since 1947.

Kempton's jumping track extends for 1 mile 5½ furlongs and includes ten stiff but fair fences; three plain ones in the home straight, a water jump, followed by a plain fence and an open ditch on the left-hand side of the triangle and four obstacles in the back stretch, the second of which is an open ditch. The fact that the run-in is short at only 175 yards and the circuit's turns are fairly tight for 'chasers means that speedy front runners, as Desert Orchid so often proved, are at a distinct advantage.

Apart from the 'King George', other prestigious jumping races staged at Kempton are the Racing Post Chase, also a 3-mile affair, and some prestigious hurdles – the 2-mile Christmas Hurdle, staged on Boxing Day, and the Lanzarote Handicap Hurdle, run if the weather permits in January.

Although a 'park' course, suburban Kempton offers racegoers an excellent view of racing. Its proximity to London makes it understandably popular.

Leicester

Leicester Racecourse
Oadby
Leicester LE2 4AL
Tel: (0116) 2716515
www.leicester-racecourse.co.uk

HOW TO GET THERE:
From North: M1 (Junct. 21); A563
From South: M1 (Junct. 21); A6
(from Kettering)
From East: A47; A427 (from
Corby); A6
From West: M54; M6 (Junct. 2);
M69; A563
By Rail: Leicester
By Air: Stoughton Airfield;
Helicopter facilities

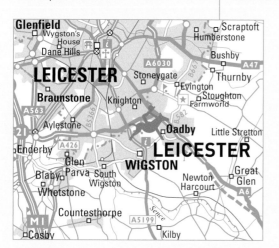

Leicester's right-handed racecourse, almost 100 miles from London, can be conveniently reached by train from St Pancras to Leicester (Midland) station where taxis and special buses provide transport to the track at Oadby two miles south-east of the city.

Motorists will find that the course, on which racing was first staged as a fully enclosed affair in the early 1880s, lies on the A6 to Market Harborough.

Some describe the shape of the circuit as a cross between a rectangle and an oval. In having a circumference of around 14 furlongs, it is a fairly extensive right-hander. Indeed, its long straight sections and well-banked bends tend to be appreciated by long-striding, galloping types, which also relish Leicester's long 4½-furlong run-in that allows jockeys to hold up their mounts in order to unleash a late challenge.

Leicester presents trainers with a welcome (since fairly rare) chance to run their charges on a perfectly straight 7 furlong 9 yard course, which is provided by a long, almost 3-furlong spur which joins the round course around 5 furlongs out. Negotiation of this particular course, which is also used for the staging of sprints, imposes a fairly stiff test of stamina since it has stretches that at times rise quite steeply before level ground is reached as the post is approached. Backers should look to performers that seem bred to stay.

On the straight course, on which sprints of 5 furlongs 2 yards and 5 furlongs 218 yards are also run, the draw is only really significant if the going is heavy and the stalls are positioned on the stands side, when low-drawn runners enjoy an edge. In races run on the round course over 9 furlongs 218 yards and 11 furlongs 183 yards, high-drawn horses enjoy a slight advantage. It is difficult to find evidence that Leicester has presented any difficulty to those who ride round its right-handed circuit. An efficient watering system prevents the going becoming too hard and, as the course drains well, its fixtures are seldom rained off.

It is also clear that the Leicester executive does its best to please those who patronize their track, since a picnic park has been provided in the silver ring and parties of ten or more racegoers who book in advance are entitled to a considerable reduction on the total cost of their admission.

The course's central location means that horseboxes from all over the country can be seen in Leicester's parking areas on race days. Indeed, this track is renowned for staging some of the biggest cards in the country and so presenting bookmakers' clerks and chalk boys with some major headaches; at the 'back end' of the flat season, a Leicester card may attract more than 120 runners. The track also stages the prestigious Leicestershire Stakes of 7 furlongs and 9 yards.

Leicester is also a National Hunt racecourse, yet its enviable situation in the heart of England's finest hunting country does not mean that those visiting it see steeplechasing at its finest. The 'chase track of ten fair, if fairly severe, fences (six in the back stretch, one just before the home turn and three in the home straight) forms a right-handed rectangle of 14 furlongs whose straight sections are extensive enough for galloping types to get into their long strides. If such runners have shown that they can race right-handed and have sufficient stamina to cope with the 3 final furlongs in which three fences have to be negotiated along with a slight elbow in the 250-yard run-in, then so much the better.

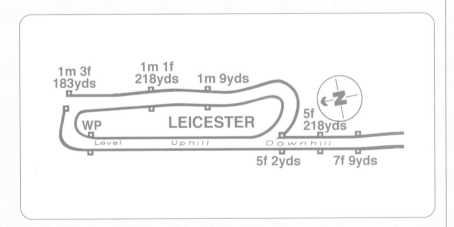

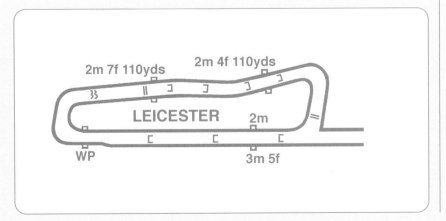

LEICESTER: Plans of the Flat course (left), and the National Hunt course (bottom).

Leicester

Leicester

Leopardstown

Ireland's equivalent of Sandown Park (it was once managed by a former assistant at this track and largely remodelled on it) is a worthy challenger for the further title of the best all-purpose course in this thoroughly horse-orientated country.

Leopardstown's magnificent new multi-million pound complex provides considerable revenue on non-race days through its sports and social facilities. On the 20 days or so when either flat or National Hunt racing takes place, crowds of up to 20,000 get a fine view of some high-class sport in enviable comfort. Leopardstown patrons can take advantage of completely enclosed facilities made up of a betting hall, four restaurants, ten bars and a dining room.

The track itself, which is the oldest of Ireland's now-dwindling number of metropolitan tracks, is a left-handed rectangle that extends for 14 furlongs. Its long straights and sweeping bends (the last of which can cause inexperienced jockeys to lose races by coming too wide) and 3-furlong run-in make it ideal for long-striding gallopers with some toe. Some believe low-drawn horses are slightly favoured on the round course.

As for the steeplechase course, this was once described by the late Pat Taaffe as better than any other in either England or Ireland. Of its 16 broad fences, which have to be negotiated in 3-mile steeplechases, the three in the back stretch are quite testing, while the going, thanks to Leopardstown's excellent natural drainage and proximity to the coast, tends to be easy. This latter advantage often means that Leopardstown is the only track in the British Isles to stage a meeting during a cold snap. Firm ground is something of a rarity, too, thanks to a most modern and extensive watering system.

Nowadays the nearest railway station (and port of disembarkation for the ferry from Holyhead) is Dún Laoghaire, which is only three miles from the course. Motorists will find Foxrock not much more than five miles from Dublin city centre, off the Stillorgan dual carriageway that links the capital with Bray.

Leopardstown has a long association with aviation (in 1955 it became the first Irish course to accommodate helicopters) and racegoers can fly in, provided they have clearance from the local Garda as well as the Racing Manager.

As one would expect of a track that was the first to feature Sunday racing and pari-mutuel-style Computote betting, Leopardstown stages some top-class flat and National Hunt racing. For example, the Irish Champion

Leopardstown Racecourse
Foxrock
Dublin 18
Ireland
Tel: 00 +353 (0)1 2893607
www.leopardstown.com

HOW TO GET THERE:

From North: N11
From South: N11
From East: R113
From West: R113
By Rail: Dún Laoghaire
By Air: Helicopter facilities

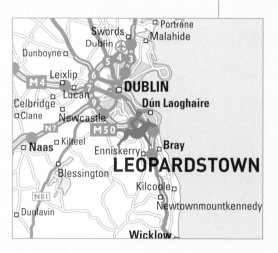

Stakes takes place over 10 furlongs in early or mid-September. A race for first-season performers, the Killavullen Stakes, staged in late October, is a mile contest confined to fillies that has on more than one occasion been won by David O'Brien.

At the four-day late December post-Christmas fixture the valuable Paddy Power Handicap Chase often falls to a seven- or eight-year-old. Proven jumpers are worth noting in the valuable Ericsson Chase, while six-year-olds often go well in the Denny's Gold Medal Novices' Chase, run over 2 miles 1 furlong.

Six-year-olds have also gone well in early January in the Pierse Handicap Hurdle (run as the Sweeps Hurdle until 1986) and in the Grade 1 A.I.G. Champion Hurdle that is contested later in the month.

Also run in early February has been the Harold Clark Handicap Chase in memory of an influential administrator, and this has often provided pointers to the Grand National, as Last Suspect proved when winning it in 1981, four years before he triumphed at Aintree at 50–1.

In February the sheer class of the 3-mile Hennessy Cognac Gold Cup steeplechase is indicated by the fact that it has often been previously captured by Cheltenham Gold Cup winners.

Many feel the facilities at Leopardstown have the ambience of a tastefully equipped and luxuriously furnished airport. No wonder then that racegoers, especially lazy ones, find the going so easy at this top-class course.

LEOPARDSTOWN: Plans of the Flat course (above), and the National Hunt course (below).

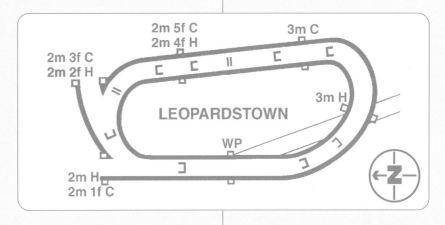

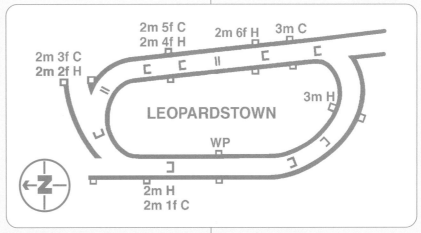

Leopardstown

Leopardstown

Limerick

Appropriately, as one of Ireland's largest cities replete with romance and history, and given its situation in the heart of some great hunting country, Limerick has its own racecourse.

This is where triple Cheltenham Gold Cup winner Cottage Rake won his first race. The track is to be found amidst the rich farming and horse-breeding area that the plains of Limerick comprise.

Established in 1916 to provide southern-based enthusiasts with yet further sport, the course is a right-handed affair with a stiff, testing climb before the turn into the finishing straight. This and two closely positioned fences in the closing stages mean that Limerick is a stayers' course. Two other reasons for this are the length of the run-in from the second last and the frequency with which the going can be soft or heavy.

Among the most important races run at Limerick are the the Munster National Chase and the intriguingly named Supermac's Hurdle and the Isle of Sky Chase .

The course is accessible from Limerick's railway station. Facilities for fixed-wing aircraft are available at Coonagh airstrip, about three miles west of Ireland's third largest city which is some 16 miles from Shannon airport. Racegoers arriving by helicopter should first seek permission to make an on-course landing by telephoning the racecourse.

Limerick Racecourse
Greenmount Park
Patrickswell
Co. Limerick
Ireland
Tel: 00 +353 (0)61 320000
www.limerick-racecourse.com

HOW TO GET THERE:
From North: R465
From South: N20
From East: N7; R503
From West: N69
By Rail: Limerick
By Air: Coonagh Aerodrome;
Helicopter facilities

LIMERICK: Plan of the course.

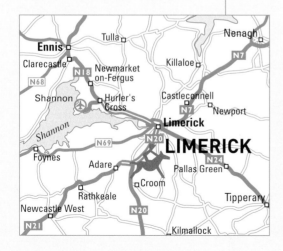

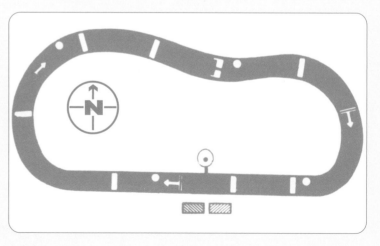

Lingfield Park

Lingfield Park Racecourse
Lingfield
Surrey RH7 6PQ
Tel: 0870 220 0022
www.lingfield-racecourse.co.uk

HOW TO GET THERE:
From North: M1 (Junct. 6A); M25 (Junct. 6); A22; B2028
From South: A23; M23 (Junct. 10); A264; A22; B2028
From East: M20 (Junct. 3); M26; M25 (Junct. 6); A22; B2028
From West: M4 (Junct. 4B); M25 (Junct. 6); A22; B2028
By Rail: Lingfield
By Air: Gatwick Airport; Helicopter facilities

Some racegoers feel that scenically Lingfield Park can rival Goodwood, although the recent redevelopment of both courses has rather reduced their aesthetic appeal. Lingfield is certainly most accessible in being only a short distance from the M23 and M25 and is well-patronized since it is less than 30 miles from London whence it can be reached conveniently by taking the M25 to junction 6, the A22 and then the B2028 after Blindley Heath. Conveniently the commuter line from London Victoria runs to Lingfield station which is only a 400-yard walk from the course.

Racing was first staged here in 1894 and since then, under various managers, many steps have been taken to attract spectators; for example, concessions for senior citizens and a very reasonable 'blanket' sum for the occupants of vehicles entering an attractive picnic park. On top of this, a Silks restaurant has recently traded on a six-day, rather than mere race day, basis, and a brasserie and cocktail bar opens its doors every night of the week.

Such innovations have meant that, with its roof-top restaurant, seafood bar, motel accommodation and exhibition centre, Lingfield has become a leisure complex for all-year-round use as well as a racecourse.

Lingfield's straight course allows races to be run over a 'short mile' of 7 furlongs 140 yards, as well as over exactly 7 furlongs and the shorter sprint distances of 5 and 6 furlongs. The ground involved descends for much of its length, sharply in fact over its first 3 furlongs or so and subsequently more gently.

Perhaps only at Epsom can a 'faster' sprint course be found.

Understandably, then, Lingfield's straight course is appreciated by fast starters, front runners and handy, sure-footed types that can keep their balance. Well-actioned animals are considered at a further advantage if allocated high numbers in the draw, especially if the stalls are positioned on the stands side. However, when it is soft or heavy underfoot, the belief is that better ground is to be found close to the far rails.

The longest races that are staged on Lingfield's straight course take place over 2 miles and are started from the 6-furlong gate. After running down the straight course for about 2 furlongs, the runners join the round course on which an important Epsom rehearsal takes place over 1 mile 3 furlongs 106 yards. This is the Derby trial that is contested in early May.

In that it consists of undulating, cambered terrain that

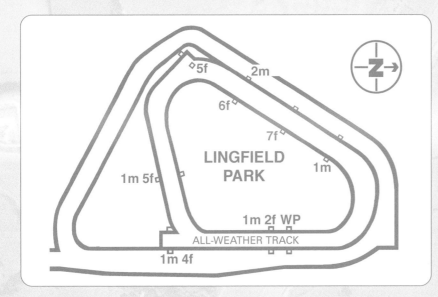

LINGFIELD PARK: Plan of the all-weather Flat course.

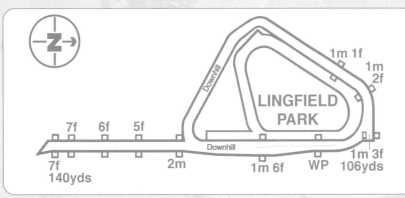

LINGFIELD PARK: Plans of the Flat turf course (top) and the National Hunt turf and all-weather course (bottom).

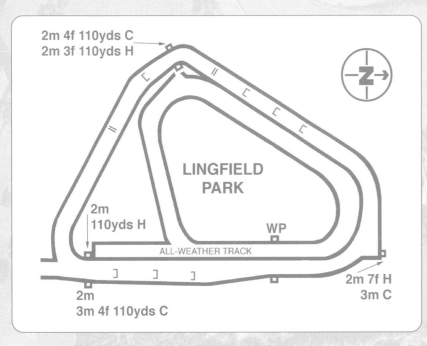

involves a slight climb out of its second turn and a steeper stretch of track, followed by a downhill run into a tightish turn into a 3-furlong-plus home straight, Lingfield's Classic Trial course, though smaller than its Epsom counterpart, does quite closely resemble it in also calling for agility and balance. It is perhaps the sharp descent into the final turn, possibly sharper than that presented by Tattenham Corner, that makes Lingfield the best simulation of the Epsom Classic experience available to trainers of Derby hopefuls. Significantly, in the 1980s three Derby winners, Teenoso, Slip Anchor and Kahyasi, had previously prevailed in Lingfield's Derby trial.

The course makes considerable demands on jockeyship and one's fancy should be partnered by a rider with an impressive wins to runs record, and the nous not to run wide around Lingfield's home turn and so throw away the chance of victory.

Past course and distance winners over 10 and 11 furlongs 106 yards often go in again at several of Lingfield's afternoon and evening fixtures. In the winter, such performers should be considered on Lingfield's jumping circuit. Shaped like a cone, it runs left-handed for around 10 furlongs and its many gradients, short 200-yard run-in and fairly demanding final four fences (of ten in all) can find out several contenders. This is why agile, hardy types with a turn of foot are to be fancied against long-striding rivals. As for hurdle races, one of these involves the quite rare distance of 23 furlongs.

In the late 1980s, Lingfield was chosen as one of two pioneering all-weather courses and its polytrack surface allows many flat race performers to race regularly in the winter. Some of the best of these contest the Winter Derby, staged at Lingfield in mid-March, a week before the flat-racing season on turf begins.

Listowel

Listowel is popular among racing scribes, no doubt largely because here in late September is staged the last of Ireland's justifiably renowned summer festival meetings. This six-day affair, linked to a local harvest festival and the all-Ireland Wren Boys competition, features a great variety of races.

As for the horse boys, they make for Listowel's island course which has been the scene of racing in this Kerry town since 1858.

The historical track, from which some splendid church spires are visible, is a rectangular flat left-hander that suits front runners and extends for over a mile and on which (if anything) high numbers are believed by some to confer an advantage. A fine view of the final two fences on the jumping circuit can be obtained from the stands.

To many, Listowel is synonymous with a marvellous atmosphere, good organization, large crowds, considerable prize money, convivial socializing, large competitive fields and heavy betting. Some important races have been the Kingdom EBF Handicap, the exotic-sounding Lartigue four-year-old handicap hurdle and, above all, the long-distance Kerry National, captured in 2002 by Monty's Pass before this gallant chaser went on to win the Grand National the following spring. The McCarthy Insurances Chase cannot offer protection to backers, but does sound a rather more sober affair than three other festival races – the Smithwicks Beer Handicap Hurdle, the Harp Lager Handicap and the Carlsberg Chase!

Listowel lies 15 miles from Tralee, from which it can be reached on the N69. Limerick-based racegoers should take the N21 to Rathkeale and then proceed along the R523. On-course car and coach parks are extensive and, unusually, free of charge – just one indication of the warm welcome extended to this popular track's many appreciative racegoers.

Listowel Racecourse
Listowel
Co. Kerry
Ireland
Tel: 00 +353 (0)68 21144

HOW TO GET THERE:
From North: N69
From South: N69
From East: N21; R523
From West: R553
By Air: Coonagh Aerodrome (approximately 50 miles from Limerick)

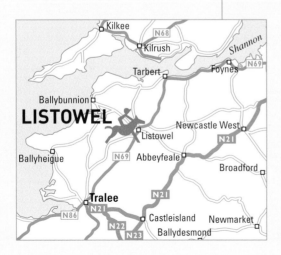

LISTOWEL: Plan of the course.

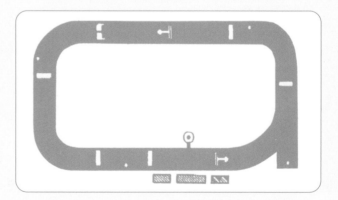

Ludlow

A list of the major races run on this delightful right-hand track reveals that the sport it offers is savoured by some connoisseurs of National Hunt racing.

Thus, a Prince of Wales Amateur Riders' Handicap Chase is annually contested and the course's upmarket ambience is further suggested by the fact that makers of a fine claret and Christies the auctioneers have each previously sponsored a steeplechase.

The fairly tight steeplechase track across the centre, which was introduced in 1870, is an oval right-hander that extends for approximately 12 furlongs.

Steeplechasers running at Ludlow can stride out reasonably well if they are not inconvenienced by having to race clockwise, jump what are eight quite stiffish fences and by finally having to slog it out on the long run-in over 200 yards to the post.

Rather unusually, the hurdle track at Ludlow, which was the original flat race course, runs outside the steeplechase course. It features undulating ground in its back stretch and extends for around a mile and a half.

Past course and distance winners well rated by stop-watch holders are often supported by knowledgeable racegoers, many of them farmers.

Racegoers can journey to this very pleasant country racecourse by taking the train to Ludlow. Then they will find the course is just a mile away on the A49 (Shrewsbury) road. This particular route is also one that should be taken by northbound travellers from Leominster and Hereford.

By prior arrangement, helicopters can land on the course, but responsibility for this proceeding must be taken by their occupants.

Some enticing sport is staged at Ludlow's many exclusively mid-week fixtures, notably the Forbra Gold Cup run in memory of the 1932 Grand National winner, which, appropriately, was owned by a retired Ludlow bookmaker.

Over the years many racegoers, some of them discerning and socially well placed, have admired the elegant ironwork on Ludlow's grandstands. In these and the course's open rooftop stand, the ruddy faces of several farmers have been seen on many a Wednesday in the jumping season. One of this select band is thrice champion National Hunt jockey Bob Davies who, as clerk of the course, does much to ensure that attractive programmes are staged on this pleasantly rural track.

The Racecourse
Bromfield
Ludlow
Shropshire SY8 2BT
Tel: (01584) 856221, 856269
www.ludlow-racecourse.co.uk

HOW TO GET THERE:

From North: A49 (from Shrewsbury)

From South: A49 (from Hereford)

From East: A456 (from Kidderminster); A49

From West: A40 (from Carmarthen); A483; A44; A49

By Rail: Ludlow

By Air: Helicopter facilities

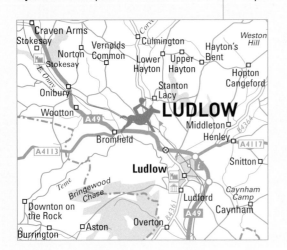

LUDLOW: Plan of the course.

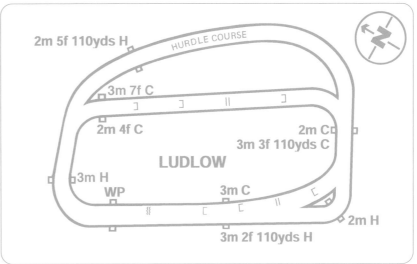

2m 5f 110yds H

HURDLE COURSE

3m 7f C

2m 4f C

2m C

3m 3f 110yds C

LUDLOW

3m H

WP

3m C

2m H

3m 2f 110yds H

Market Rasen

Market Rasen Racecourse
Legsby Road
Market Rasen
Lincolnshire LN8 3EA
Tel: (01673) 843434
www.marketrasenraces.co.uk

HOW TO GET THERE:
From North: A1; A46 (from Grimsby)
From South: A46 (from Lincoln)
From East: A631 (from Louth)
From West: A631 (from Gainsborough)
By Rail: Market Rasen
By Air: Wickenby Flying Club; Helicopter pad

Picturesquely situated in the Wolds and the only racecourse in Lincolnshire, Market Rasen is well managed and has enjoyed the distinction of closing the 'main' National Hunt season.

The track itself is a right-handed oval of 10 furlongs and features slight undulations for much of its extent. Its bends are fairly sharp and the last of these into the home straight features a slight decline; thus in the wet some runners find its negotiation difficult.

The jumping circuit contains eight fences, four in the back stretch and four in the home straight. These are far from testing and so Market Rasen usually suits handy speedsters who find no difficulty in coping with its clockwise configuration. Previous course winners are always worth consideration, while the short run-in of around a furlong tends to suit front runners.

Many meetings are held in the summer when the course's picnic area is greatly appreciated by family groups of racegoers, some of whom motor 160 miles from London. Most of the summer race days take place at weekends and the highlight of these is the summer place meeting in late July.

The course is 16 miles north-east of Lincoln and a mile east of the town of Market Rasen. Those travelling north-east from Lincoln should take the A46, as should travellers coming off the A1 from the south. The A631 will serve many racegoers from Yorkshire and this, the 'racecourse road' itself (to Louth), can be joined from the M18 (Junction 4).

Market Rasen station (which is a mile from the course) can be reached from London King's Cross via Newark, while air travellers may be able to make landings at Wickenby Flying Club, five miles away to the south.

MARKET RASEN: Plan of the course.

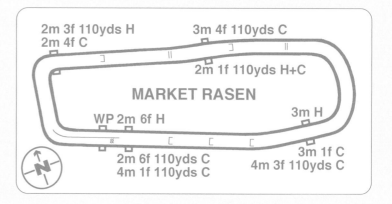

Musselburgh

Formerly Edinburgh, this racecourse is at Musselburgh, five miles or so from the Scottish capital in a maritime location on the Firth of Forth.

It can be reached by rail by taking an express from King's Cross to Edinburgh's impressive Waverley station whence a 'super sprinter' service can be taken to Musselburgh itself. Motorists travelling from the south should take the Great North Road (A1).

The track, with its natural sandy subsoil and sometimes windy situation close to the Muirfield golf course, is one on which sticky conditions are seldom found. It is an oval right-hander of over 10 furlongs that features occasional, very minor undulations and has a straight run-in of 4 furlongs. However, it does not really suit long-striding, galloping types, since its turns, despite being cambered, are tight, especially into the finishing straight. Handy, adaptable types, preferably high-drawn ones that have shown a liking for racing the 'wrong way', often go well in races of 7 furlongs 30 yards, 1 mile 16 yards and 12 furlongs 31 yards, all of these being race distances that

Musselburgh Racecourse
Linkfield Road
Musselburgh
East Lothian
Scotland EH21 7RG
Tel: (0131) 665 2859

HOW TO GET THERE:
From North: A9; M90 (Junct. 1); A90; A902; A199
From South: M6; M74; A702; A720
From East: A1 (from Dunbar)
From West: M8 (Junct. 1); A720
By Rail: Waverley
By Air: Edinburgh; Helicopter facilities

take in much of Musselburgh's round course. Indeed, if jockeys do not take their mounts the shortest way round this, they can lose many lengths, a sound reason for following jockeys with impressive wins to rides ratios.

The straight course, on which 5-furlong sprints are staged, features flat ground in its final furlong. When the stalls are placed on the stands side, low-drawn contenders enjoy an appreciable edge, but if these are positioned on the far side, high-drawn runners are at a slight advantage. All in all, the sprint course is not so idiosyncratic as to impose anything but an easy test. A horse that can break quickly from the stalls is often favoured.

Although not a purpose-built, all-weather jumping track, Musselburgh is Britain's nearest natural equivalent to this. Victory often goes to fleet-footed types who are adaptable and can readily negotiate the many tight turns that have to be encountered in National Hunt contests run round the 11-furlong track.

The racecourse has led a charmed life, having twice been saved – first by Lord Roseberry as senior steward and then by the building of the Forth Road Bridge.

MUSSELBURGH: Plans of the Flat course (top) and the National Hunt course (bottom).

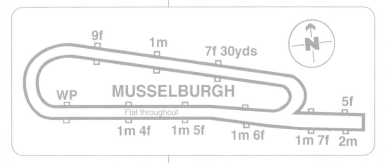

Naas

Some 21 miles from Dublin can be found the chief town of Kildare, the busy industrial centre of Naas which is Gaelic for 'assembly'. This is one of the former seats of the Kings of Leinster.

Ever since 1924, Naas, with its left-handed configuration, uphill finish and long run-in, has been known as the 'backer's graveyard'. This is primarily because it saps the stamina of irresolute runners.

Whilst no extremely prestigious races are run on this dual-purpose demanding track, plenty of interest has been generated by the Naas Ni Riogh Novice Steeplechase, the Slaney Hurdle, the Johnstown Novice Hurdle, the Brown Lad Handicap Hurdle (run in honour of the three-times winner of the Irish Grand National), the Woodlands Park Novice Chase, the Swordlestown Stud Sprint (the richest two-year-old listed fillies' race in Europe), the Garnet Stakes, the Birdcatcher Nursery and the Poplar Square Chase.

The last-mentioned is often won by a 'pigeon catcher', while some racegoers have looked for a runner with a suitably eloquent name in the Racing Writers' Perpetual Trophy Hurdle.

Since Naas lies on the N7 dual carriageway from Dublin, it enjoys excellent accessibility. Hot beef rolls are available and these form a fraction of the excellent catering, some of which is available in a panoramic restaurant that, along with a new grandstand and indoor Tote betting hall, greatly enhanced the facilities on offer when they were built in 1998. Phase 2 of an on-going development plan will include state-of-the-art arrangements for both racegoers and many of racing's varied workforce. During the summer the 'craic' at Naas features live music on the green.

Naas Racecourse
Tipper Road
Naas
Co. Kildare
Ireland
Tel: 00 +353 (0)45 897391
www.naasracecourse.com

HOW TO GET THERE:
From North: R409
From South: N9
From East: N7
From West: N7
By Air: Dublin Airport (approximately 20 miles from Dublin)

NAAS: Plan of the course.

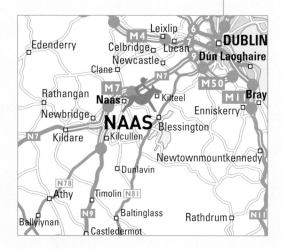

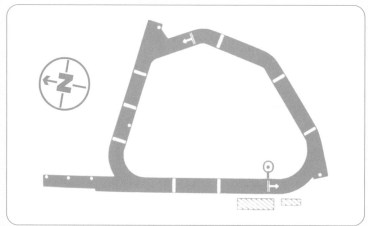

Newbury

An important Group event, the John Porter Stakes, run at just over 1½ miles at Newbury's first April meeting, commemorates the famous nineteenth-century trainer to whom this left-handed course owes its existence, thanks partly to the encouragement of King Edward VII. Porter was in retirement when the track he had dreamed of came into being on 26 September 1905.

Its excellent conformation and proximity both to the major training centres of Berkshire and Wiltshire and to London just over 60 miles away have meant that, from the first, Newbury has been popular with racing's professionals.

The fact that large fields and good ground can virtually be guaranteed at Newbury is a further tribute to Porter's inspired vision. Although the track saw service in the Second World War as a railway marshalling yard and its straight course was altered in time for the 1956 season, it has largely survived in its original form.

Newbury can almost be regarded as a racecourse custom-built to put the ability of top-class thoroughbreds fully, but fairly, on trial. This is why so many two-year-olds are given their introductions to racing here, why defeat at Newbury is so seldom blamed on the track and form from this particular course tends to work out well.

The track itself consists of a left-handed oval whose circumference extends for almost 1 mile 7 furlongs. Its long, wide straights, since they feature occasional rather mild undulations, are appreciated by long-striding gallopers. If the strong suit of such animals is stamina, they find Newbury greatly to their liking since its gentle bends can be taken at a good gallop.

The longest races staged at Newbury take place over 2 miles and are started a furlong from the winning post in front of the grandstand that horses run past as they make their finishing efforts. Since such events involve four left-hand turns, they confer an understandable if none-too-pronounced advantage on lowly drawn runners (as do, of course, shorter races of about 7 furlongs, about 1 mile, 10 furlongs 6 yards, 11 furlongs 5 yards, 12 furlongs 5 yards, and 1 mile 5 furlongs 61 yards, that are also run on the round course). The first turn, like its successors a fairly gentle affair, is negotiated by those tackling 2 miles soon after they have raced across the finishing line. (Incidentally, a short spur projecting from the top of the next bend allows races over 1 mile 5 furlongs 61 yards.)

The long back straight on the round course, along which starting stalls are positioned to allow races to be contested

Newbury Racecourse
Newbury
Berkshire RG14 7NZ
Tel: (01635) 40015
www.newbury-racecourse.co.uk

HOW TO GET THERE:
From North: A34 (from Oxford)
From South: A34 (from Winchester)
From East: M4 (Junct. 12); A4
From West: M20 (Junct. 3); M26; M25 (Junct. 5); M4 (Junct. 13); A34
By Rail: Newbury Racecourse
By Air: Light aircraft and helicopter facilities

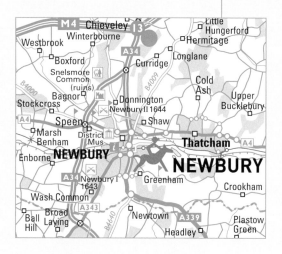

over 12 furlongs 5 yards, 11 furlongs 5 yards and 10 furlongs 6 yards, is fairly level, the only significant undulations occurring just before it leads into another left-hand bend.

Every horse that races on the round course encounters gently descending ground as it approaches the easy home turn and once in the home straight finds itself on a run-in that takes in most of the 5-furlong sprint course which features slight undulations throughout. This gives jockeys on horses that need to be held up a golden opportunity to poach the lead close to home from horses that have made their finishing efforts earlier.

Newbury's straight mile track on which, if anything, high-drawn runners are favoured, especially in the wet if fields are large and the stalls positioned on the stands side or in the centre of the course, is a full 90 feet wide and is partly provided by the longest of the three spurs that project from the round course. It is used to stage several important pattern events. One, the Juddmonte Lockinge Stakes, in which four-year-olds often go well, takes place over its full length in mid-May. In addition, a 2000 Guineas Trial (the Greenham Stakes) is started from the 7-furlong gate in April.

One important 6 furlong 8 yard race for top-class two-year-olds that takes place on the straight course in September is the Mill Reef Stakes, named after the Derby and Arc de Triomphe winner of 1971.

Several top-class races are also run on Newbury's round course. These include three prestigious races that are run over the 7 furlong course. In April, three-year-old fillies contest the Fred Darling Stakes, which commemorates the famous Beckhampton trainer who sent out seven Derby winners. Others are the Horris Hill Stakes, an important test of stamina for two-year-olds in late October, and the Hungerford Stakes in August.

Some longer prestigious events are staged on the round course. The longest is the Geoffrey Freer Stakes run over 1 mile 5 furlongs 61 yards, also in mid-August, in memory of a Newbury clerk of the course. A 'pattern' race, the St Simon Stakes, run over 12 furlongs 5 yards in late October, is

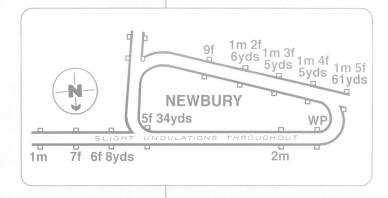

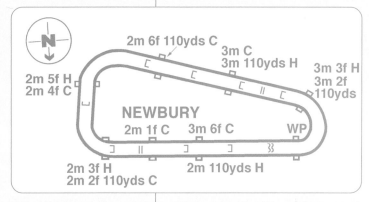

NEWBURY: Plans of the Flat course (top), over which the Juddmonte Lockinge Stakes and the Greenham Stakes (a 2000 Guineas Trial) are run, and the National Hunt course (bottom) over which the Tote Gold Trophy and Hennessy Cognac Gold Cup take place.

also something of a three-year-olds' benefit and commemorates an unbeaten colt whose progeny also proved very successful.

The gravel in the subsoil beneath Newbury's luxuriant and springy turf ensures that heavy ground is something of a rarity. What is more, the sting can be taken out of firm ground by Newbury's modern and highly sophisticated watering system.

Naturally, Newbury draws a large number of its racegoers from London. Trains take around an hour from Paddington to reach the racecourse station that is a three-minute walk away from the track itself; very attractive deals involving travel and admission are available.

Newbury's popularity owes much to its accessibility, the first-class view from its six-level Berkshire stand, its new Racegoers' grandstand and the fact that its admission charges are so reasonable.

As a premier venue for National Hunt racing, Newbury imposes a searching, but very fair test for jumpers. The trace is 80 feet wide and its considerable extent of about 15 furlongs makes it decidedly 'galloping' in nature.

The jumping circuit has easy bends, undulates in places and features 11 fences (five in each straight and one tricky cross fence before the home run) that are on the stiff side of fair. The four in the 5-furlong finishing straight can impose quite a severe test of courage, stamina and jumping ability, especially when the going is soft or heavy.

Past winners of 'chases and hurdles are often worthy of further consideration, as are runners that have gone well previously at other 'galloping' tracks like Haydock Park, Worcester, Doncaster or Ayr.

Newbury's first big jumping race is the Hennessy Cognac Gold Cup, a handicap steeplechase run over 3 miles 2½ furlongs in late November. Previously won by stars such as Arkle and Burrough Hill Lad, this is often lifted by a seven-year-old.

The Tote (formerly Schweppes) Gold Trophy is an early February hurdle race in which some heavy betting usually takes place.

Newbury's even earlier, popular, late-December fixture features the Mandarin Chase, a 26-furlong-plus affair that commemorates the 1962 Cheltenham Gold Cup winner.

Newcastle

An impressive racecourse is to be found in an attractive 1000-acre setting at High Gosforth Park, five miles north of Newcastle upon Tyne, whose associations with horseracing date back to the early 1600s.

The present course was first used in 1882 as a replacement for the Town Moor site on which racing (including the now defunct Newcastle Gold Cup) was originally staged within the city limits. Newcastle is renowned as the home of the Northumberland Plate, which was first staged on Town Moor as a relatively modest 2-mile handicap in 1833. Although it no longer attracts such high-class animals, this 'Pitmen's Derby', as it is popularly known, still attracts a huge crowd when it is staged as the highlight of Newcastle's late June meeting. Still run over 2 miles 19 yards, it is often captured by a four-year-old.

The Newcastle course is a broad left-handed, rather pear-shaped oval that has a circumference of 14 furlongs. All those who race over it, be it on the straight or the round course, have to negotiate a final stretch of around 4 furlongs that rises slightly but relentlessly until the distance. This helps to make Newcastle a testing track that makes considerable demands on a horse's courage, stamina and resolution, especially if it is a two-year-old having an early-season run on heavy going.

Runners in the Northumberland Plate and other 2 mile 19 yard contests race entirely on the round course. They start to race about 2 furlongs out; then, after passing the winning post and Newcastle's well-appointed stands, they run round the first of three bends which, because they are particularly well-banked, can be taken at stamina-sapping speed and tend to reduce the advantage that following a left-handed running rail accords the lowly drawn. After passing the 1 mile 4 furlong 93 yard gate, those on the round course encounter a second left-hand bend from which a spur projects to permit the staging of races run over 10 furlongs 32 yards. This spur is a short affair that leads into a longish stretch along which, from appropriate points, races over 9 furlongs 9 yards and mile events are started.

The round course climbs slightly as it approaches the home turn, another well-banked affair that can be taken at speed and which runs into the straight course. This actually extends for 8 furlongs and 3 yards. The straight course is mainly used to stage sprints and 7-furlong

Newcastle Racecourse
High Gosforth Park
Newcastle upon Tyne NE3 5HP
Tel: (0191) 236 2020
www.newcastleracecourse.co.uk

HOW TO GET THERE:
From North: A1; B1318
From South: A1(M); B1318
From East: A1058 (from Tynemouth)
From West: A69; A1; B1318
By Rail: Newcastle Central, (5 miles); Four Lane Ends Metro; (free bus service to course)
By Air: Newcastle International Airport; Helicopter facilities

events. For the most part the ground on the straight course rises steadily until some 200 yards from the post, thus imposing a severe test of stamina that only the resolute and powerful galloper and the tough two-year-old are likely to relish.

As for the draw, in straight-course races of 5 to 7 furlongs, when the stalls are on the stands side, the highly drawn are favoured. However, if there is some cut in the ground, the advantage switches to the lowly drawn. If the stalls are placed in the centre or far side, low numbers are those to look out for in draw allocations, especially if soft or heavy conditions prevail. A low draw is coveted in such conditions as the high drawn have to waste valuable time switching to the far side of the straight where the ground rides a good deal firmer and faster.

The Newcastle course is one on which the abilities of top-class thoroughbreds can be fully tested. Not surprisingly, therefore, it is used to stage a number of important races.

Newcastle's only Group race is the B6 furlong John Smith's Extra Smooth Chipchase Stakes run on the straight course in late June.

Newcastle owes much of its popularity to the enterprise and energy of its far-sighted executive which has repeatedly demonstrated its concern for the welfare of both the racing public and those responsible for the horses that come to Gosforth. In fact, it pioneered the provision of proper accommodation for stable staff and most commendably, not long ago, spent several thousand pounds on improving facilities for female horse attendants.

With its escalators, betting halls, attractive restaurants and modern well-heated stands, Newcastle calls to mind certain American and Australian tracks. Younger racegoers are encouraged to sample the delights of the unusual adventure playground.

Even on non-racing days, Newcastle's sporting and social facilities are in constant demand. The site is home to the permanent headquarters of the Boy Scout Association in Northumberland and also boasts a wildlife sanctuary.

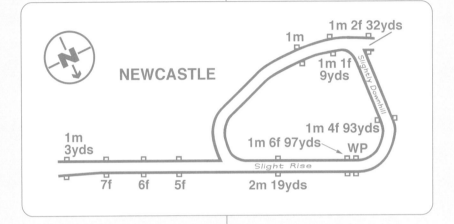

NEWCASTLE: Plan of the course

Newcastle

The proximity of the track to major northern population centres provides a further guarantee that good crowds can pass through its turnstiles. Fortunately, as the course is readily accessible to those who live beyond Tyneside, it attracts many southern trainers. There is a helicopter landing pad near the water jump on the steeplechasing course, while fixed-wing aircraft can be accommodated at Newcastle International Airport some six miles away. Newcastle is easily reached by air from Heathrow or Gatwick or by rail to Newcastle Central from London King's Cross. Rail travellers should take the Metro to Four Lane Ends and then make a bus journey to Gosforth.

The A1 by passes the nearby city and runs close to the course which adjoins the B1318. There are free parking facilities.

As one of the North's top National Hunt venues, Newcastle stages some good-quality racing. This takes place on a pear-shaped, left-handed jumping circuit whose circumference is 14 furlongs. It is renowned for the stiffness of its eleven fences and the thoroughly testing nature of its steadily ascending home stretch of 4 furlongs.

Thus, proven stayers and sound jumpers should be sought at Newcastle. Those with a touch of class are often aimed at the Fighting Fifth Hurdle that is staged in late November. A win in this is often registered by a hurdler of Cheltenham championship standard.

The Eider Handicap Chase is a most enticing and thrilling marathon race of 4 miles 1 furlong that (weather permitting) is staged at Gosforth in February. Often rightly regarded as providing revealing pointers to the Grand National prospects, it is a favourite with local racegoers.

Newmarket

Newmarket Racecourses
Westfield House, The Links
Newmarket
Suffolk CB8 0TG
Tel: (01638) 663482
www.newmarketracecourses.co.uk

HOW TO GET THERE:
From North: A1(M); A14; A1304
From South: A11; M11 (Junct. 9);
A1304
From East: A14 (from Bury St
Edmunds); A1304
From West: A14 (from Kettering);
A1304
By Rail: Cambridge (13 miles);
Newmarket (limited service);
courtesy bus from station and High
Street to racecourse and return
By Air: Cambridge Airport;
Course airstrip

As the home and 'headquarters' of British flat racing, Newmarket deserves a lengthy entry. The course is as appealing as the Suffolk town of which it forms a distinct part.

Newmarket's two courses, the Rowley Mile course and the July course, form the arms of a huge Y-shaped track that imposes the best tests of thoroughbred racehorses that are available anywhere.

It is perfectly straight and extremely wide; indeed, in modern times only half of it has been used for racing, in contrast to the time when Charles II became the first (and so far the only) reigning monarch to ride a flat race winner. The Rowley Mile course (on which the only draw advantage involves low-drawn horses in races from 5 to 8 furlongs when the ground is soft) is reasonably flat in its early stages, but at a natural landmark around 2 furlongs out (which for obvious reasons is called 'the bushes') the ground dips for a furlong. Next comes a furlong or so of rising ground that continues to the line. The fact that as they emerge out of 'the dip' the runners can see rising ground extending for 3 furlongs well beyond the winning post (which may not be perceived and whose significance is lost on them) is one reason why so many turn it in at this critical point in their races.

The first meeting that takes place on the 10-furlong Rowley Mile course (which also caters for long distances by taking in the 'tail' of Newmarket's Y-shaped configuration, provided by the so-called Beacon or Cesarewitch course, and also a right-handed bend) is staged in mid-April. One of its highlights (often captured by a subsequent 1000 Guineas winner) is the 7-furlong Nell Gwyn Stakes, run in memory of Charles II's mistress whose quarters were connected by a subterranean passage with his Newmarket Palace. This arrangement is also recalled by the King Charles II Stakes, yet another Group race that is staged at the end of May.

As for the 2000 Guineas Trial, Newmarket also stages, at an early point in the season, the 1 mile Craven Stakes. In recent years this has been won by such runners as Shadeed, Dancing Brave, Doyoun and Tirol that have gone on to achieve Classic success over the course and distance some two weeks later.

Both the 2000 and 1000 Guineas, the most prestigious races run on the Rowley Mile course, are contested at Newmarket's second spring meeting that takes place in late April or early May. French and Irish stables make particularly determined bids to capture the former, such is its kudos, while the latter is sometimes landed by a previously successful trainer.

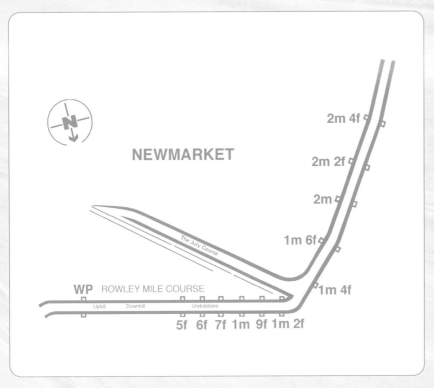

NEWMARKET: Plans of the Rowley Mile course (top), and the July course (bottom).

The two courses form the arms of a huge Y-shaped track that imposes the best tests of thoroughbred racehorses available anywhere.

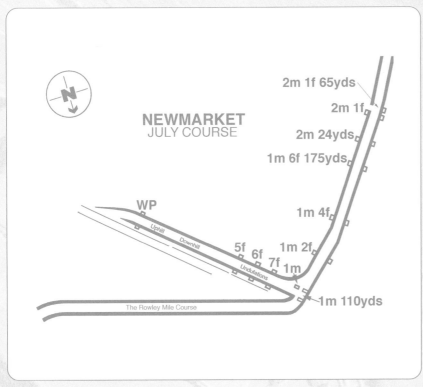

Also run at the second spring meeting is an historic race with strong Jockey Club connections. This, restricted to horses owned by members of the Jockey Club or the Jockey Club rooms, is the Newmarket Challenge Whip and the trophy awarded to the winner of this 1 mile contest for three-year-old maidens is said to contain hair from the famous past champion, Eclipse.

The programme for Newmarket's second three-day fixture is arranged so that before the season's first two Classics the Jockey Club Stakes is contested – most appropriately since Newmarket is where the headquarters of racing's administrators has long been located. Run over the closing stages of the Beacon course and thus soon involving a right-hand bend into the 10 furlongs of the Rowley Mile, this 12-furlong race is a top-class, early season contest for four-year-olds and upwards and in its time has been captured by some previous Derby winners (St Paddy in 1961 for example) and by horses like Ardross that have gone on to win the Ascot Gold Cup.

The July course which, like the rest of the Newmarket track, was initially laid out with horsemen and not spectators in mind, is nonetheless blessed with picturesque thatched buildings and its delightfully leafy paddock offers some welcome shade in the summer months. This particular course allows races to be run over 1 mile, 7 furlongs and sprint distances. It is straight, but after 2 furlongs some descending ground is encountered until the distance. The final furlong consists of rising terrain.

As it does for the Rowley Mile course, the Beacon course allows the July course to figure in the closing stages of longish races of 10 and 12 furlongs, 1 mile 6 furlongs and around 170 yards and 2 miles 24 yards.

Some prestigious and historic races are staged on the July course. An early example is the 12-furlong Prince of Wales' Stakes. First run in 1894, this is a race in which three- and four-year-olds understandably go well.

Also run at the first July meeting are three important 6-furlong sprints. The first to be staged is the Cherry Hinton Stakes for two-year-old fillies, while the second is the colts' equivalent, the July Stakes, first run as long ago as 1786. Then comes the third: the July Cup, an all-aged sprint of championship class, in which three-year-olds have the best record.

With the coming of autumn, the Rowley Mile course is again pressed into service and in early October the first major race involved in proceedings is another two-year-old 6-furlong dash – the Cheveley Park Stakes, in which French and Irish raiders should always be respected.

Another top-class, 6-furlong juvenile contest that is run on the second day of the first October meeting is the Middle Park Stakes, the result of which can produce a major shake-up in the long-range, ante-post betting on the following season's Classics. Seldom, however, in recent seasons has the winner of this race gone on to win the 2000 Guineas some six months or so later, Right Tack, Brigadier Gerard and Rodrigo de Triano being some exceptions.

NEWMARKET:
The National Stud

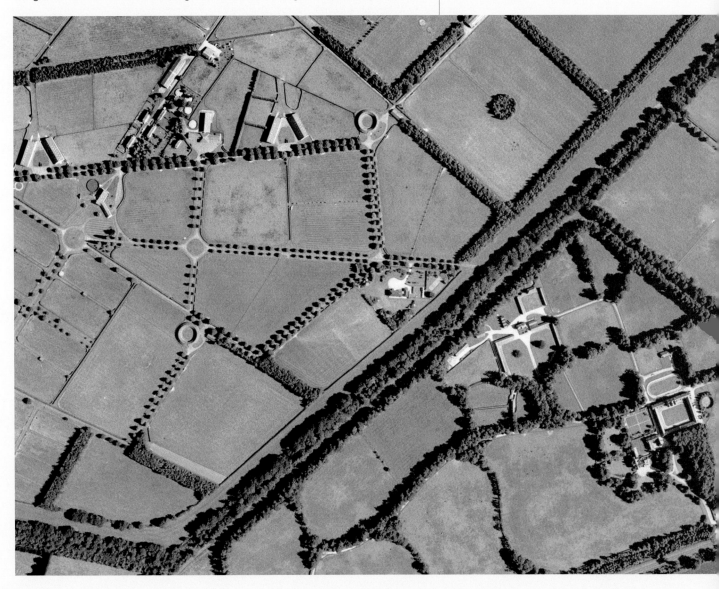

A longer race run at this meeting is the Sun Chariot Stakes, named after King George VI's Triple Crown winner of 1942. This is an 8-furlong race for fillies and mares which, since it became an all-aged affair in 1974, has often fallen to a three-year-old.

The best-known race run at the first October meeting is the historic Cambridgeshire, a highly competitive handicap run at a blistering pace over 9 furlongs of Newmarket's heathland. This is often won by a gutsy contender with indomitable courage that can stay 10 furlongs, rather than a mile or even 9 furlongs on less taxing terrain elsewhere.

As for the second leg of the Autumn Double, the Cesarewitch, this is the gambling highlight of the second October meeting. A race in which fillies do not have an impressive record, it takes place over twice the distance of the Cambridgeshire: 18 gruelling furlongs of featureless heathland which includes what Richard Onslow has called a 'stark staring straight' of more than a mile. The majority of past winners have been three- or four-year-olds, with the latter having the best record. Understandably, runners carrying less than 8 stone often enjoy an edge in such a long race. Rank outsiders can generally be disregarded, but not lightly raced types. Horses fresh from having been rested should be noted, as should any runner that has scored over 2 miles earlier in the season.

The Challenge Stakes is a late-season Newmarket Group race that since 1976 has been run over 7, rather than 6, furlongs. Three-year-olds have the best record here.

Future 2000 Guineas prospects can advertise their claims in the Dewhurst Stakes, as did its 1983, 1992 and 1994 winners: El Gran Senor, Zafonic and Pennekamp, respectively. The Dewhurst often features a strong and sometimes successful Irish challenge.

Also run at Newmarket in October is the Rockfel Stakes, another 7-furlong race confined to two-year-old fillies. It commemorates the 1938 winner of the 1000 Guineas, Oaks and Champion Stakes. The last-named is, in fact, the last major race of the season that is staged at racing's headquarters and an event in which some past winners of the 2000 and 1000 Guineas have understandably prevailed.

Newmarket is a connoisseur's choice of a racecourse, with ample free parking available for both cars and coaches and a fine adventure playground on both the Rowley Mile and the July course which is currently staffed by Red Cross personnel. Facilities were improved even further in 2000 with the construction of the Millennium stand. Newmarket is accessible by train from London

King's Cross, but only via a limited service to what is an unmanned halt. Indeed, such are the difficulties rail travellers can face that on race days, a coach operates from the station at Cambridge some 13 miles away. This city is also accessible by air via Cambridge Airport. Given Newmarket's vast acreage, it is not surprising that this includes a 1000-metre grass airstrip.

Motorists arriving from London (about 60 miles away) arrive via the M11, leaving at Junction 9 before travelling on to the course via the A11 and then the A1303 or A1304.

However they arrive at this 'HQ', many racegoers combine their visit to Newmarket with a chance to savour what the town also has to offer by way of stables, studs, museums, bookshops and excellent training grounds.

Newton Abbot

Summer holidays would hardly be the same without the six Newton Abbot fixtures that take place in July and August.

Given its proximity to the resort of Torquay, there is often a festive atmosphere at this Devon course, which is attractive to both racing professionals and to holidaymakers.

The almost square-shaped circuit of only 9 furlongs is so tight it contains a mere seven fences which, save for the second in the far straight, cause most runners few problems, although they cannot be so easily skipped over as was once the case.

The sheer tightness of the track and its very short run-in of about 300 yards from the last obstacle means that it tends to suit nippy, front-running types. Previous course winners often relish a further chance to race round its tight, left-handed turns.

Those who take the train from London Paddington to Newton Abbot can either take a taxi or walk a mere mile to the course itself, while motorists should leave the nearby M5 at junction 31 and look for signs soon indicating the A380 (Torquay) road. Those arriving from the west can take the A38 from Plymouth.

Some feel the course's proximity to an industrial estate detracts from its general location in some delightfully scenic Devon countryside. However, the view of the racing on offer is excellent. Newton Abbot is also popular with many jockeys.

Newton Abbot Racecourse
Kingsteighton Road
Newton Abbot
Devon TQ12 3AF
Tel: (01626) 353235

HOW TO GET THERE:
From North: M5 (Junct. 31); A38; A380
From South: A38; A380
From East: A381
From West: A38 (from Plymouth); A383
By Rail: Newton Abbot
By Air: Exeter airport; Helicopter facilities

NEWTON ABBOT: Plan of the course.

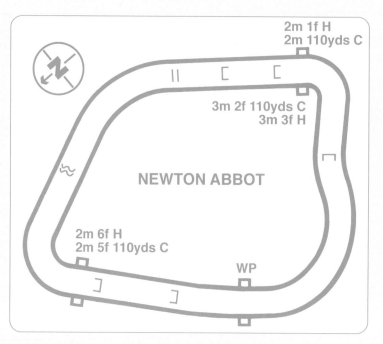

Nottingham

Nottingham Racecourse
Colwick Park
Nottingham NG2 4BE
Tel: (0115) 958 0620
www.nottinghamracecourse.co.uk

HOW TO GET THERE:
From North: M1 (Junct. 26)
From South: M1 (Junct. 25)
From East: A52
From West: A50 (from Stoke-on-Trent)
N.B. In Nottingham follow 'Football and Cricket Traffic' signs, eventually picking up brown 'Nottingham Racecourse' signs and yellow park-and-ride signs. The course is on the B686 which can be reached from the A52/A6011 or the A612.
By Rail: Nottingham Midland
By Air: East Tollerton Airport; Helicopter facilities

Properly organized horseracing has taken place on the Nottingham site where it is currently staged since August 1892. Unlike its predecessor, which was owned by the local corporation, the present racecourse is administered and leased by a private concern, the Racecourse Holding Trust. It is to be found less than two miles east of Nottingham's railway station (accessible from London St Pancras) at Colwick Park. This can be reached by M1 travellers from junction 25 or 26, from which access can eventually be gained to the course via the B686 Colwick road. Those flying in by helicopter can be accommodated on course, while fixed-winged aircraft can land at Tollerton two miles away.

As for the track itself, it is a left-handed, mainly level affair of approximately 12 furlongs in extent; its negotiation presents good horses with little difficulty as the only undulations it features are minor ones.

Such animals can quite often be seen in action at Nottingham since potentially top-class two-year-olds from the yards of leading Newmarket handlers often make their debuts here in what are very fair and relatively undemanding circumstances. What is more, sprinters that have previously been considered good enough to take their chances in Goodwood's Stewards' Cup sometimes contest Nottingham's far from humble equivalent, a 6 furlong 15 yard handicap run at Colwick Park in early August.

The circuit is appreciated by powerful, galloping types for its long straights and fairly gentle left-hand bends. Furthermore, if jockeys are instructed to come with a late run they will find the 4½-furlong run-in ideal for such tactics.

A spur projecting from the final bend on the round course allows races to be run over 5 furlongs 13 yards and 6 furlongs 15 yards along a section of track that can be taken at speed since it is straight and mainly flat.

Experts maintain that runners allotted high numbers enjoy an advantage in these races, especially when the stalls are placed on the stands rails and the going is soft. If the stalls are on the far side and the going good to firm, low-drawn horses are favoured.

Marathons take place at Colwick Park over 2 miles 9 yards and 2 miles 2 furlongs and 18 yards. After leaving stalls positioned around 4½ furlongs from the post, those tackling 2 miles race over virtually the full length of the run-in. Subsequently, they run round the rather semi-circular far turn, past the 9 furlong 213 yard start and then enter Nottingham's flat and fairly lengthy mild dog leg of a back straight whose kink involves the point from which races over 1 mile 54 yards start. Thereafter, the racecourse involves a second, gentler left-hand bend, before it joins the straight course 4½ furlongs out. As a left-handed course, Nottingham confers a slight advantage on low-drawn runners.

By setting aside a special, rather scenic parking area on the rails and charging up to four occupants of a car a single reduced rate to enter it, the Nottingham executive have enticed many members of the public to take a picnic and go racing in Colwick Park.

NOTTINGHAM: Plan of the Flat course.

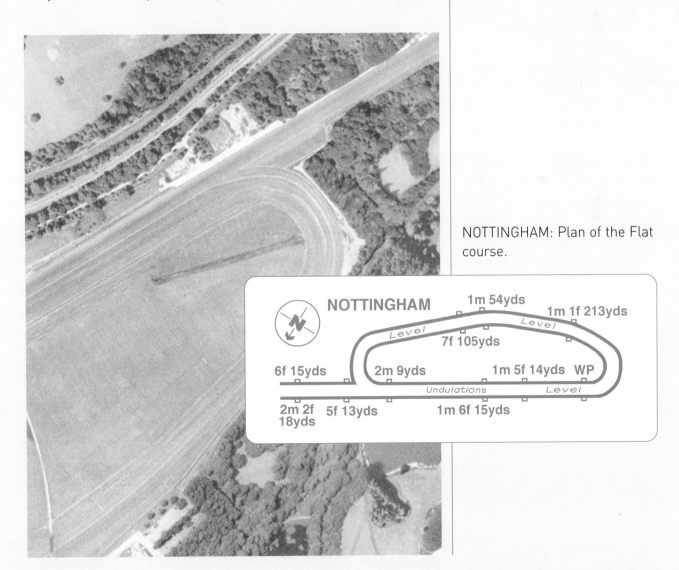

Nottingham

Nottingham

Perth

There is no more northerly track in Britain than Perth racecourse, which is most picturesque in being set in the wooded parkland that makes up the grounds of Scone Palace.

The fact that it is alternatively known as 'Perth Hunt' provides a hint of the Corinthian and very sporting flavour of the action that takes place here, before and after the ravages of a Scottish winter.

The track lies three miles north of Perth just off the A93 and can be reached by those travelling from the Edinburgh via the M90. Perth station is accessible by rail from London's King's Cross some 450 miles away. Racegoers who wish to fly should land at Perth aerodrome some three miles away, but only after telephoning and booking a taxi to be on hand at their estimated time of arrival. There is also a car-hire service.

As for the course, it is a mainly flat, rather oblong-shaped right-hander of 10 furlongs in extent. Its eight fences are not as easy as some have claimed and, interestingly, the water jump is omitted in steeplechases on the final circuit. A run on this track is relished by nippy, adaptable horses who can handle its sharp bends and get into a longish lead by the time the 300-yard run-in has to be negotiated.

As much as the excellent view from the stands, most racegoers appreciate Perth's rustic charm that is epitomized by its old-fashioned grandstand, in which good crowds of friendly local hunt members are joined by visitors, many of whom take advantage of the fact that many meetings here are two- or three-day affairs.

Perth now has a new stand, the 'Dewhurst', which is well patronized, as are a number of private marquee facilities.

Perth Racecourse
Scone Palace Park
Perth PH2 6BB
Tel: (01738) 551597
www.perth-races.co.uk

HOW TO GET THERE:
From North: A93 (from Braemar); A9 (from Pitlochry)
From South: M90 (Junct. 11)
From East: A90 (from Dundee)
From West: A85 (from Oban)
By Rail: Perth (free bus service to course)
By Air: Scone airstrip

PERTH: Plan of the course.

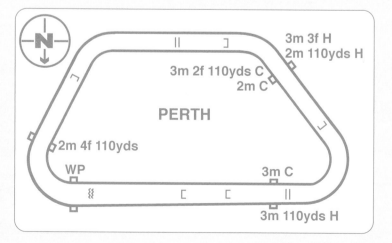

Plumpton

So tricky do some jockeys consider Plumpton that they are reluctant to race on it. However, this extreme view is not generally held, which is fortunate since the sport staged on this Sussex track is very popular, particularly among bank holiday picnickers.

The course, which has a definite country feel to it, lies north-east of Brighton whence motorists can take the A27 to Lewes, join the A275 north of this town and then the B2116.

Rail travellers can journey from London Victoria to Plumpton station, which is a short walk away from the course. Helicopters can land on the course, after first obtaining permission.

As a racecourse, Plumpton is a left-hand, tight, undulating rectangular track of only 9 furlongs. Thus, understandably, there are only a handful of fences, two of which, on the far side, can cause several runners to come to grief. The run-in is short at only 200 yards – a further reason why this is a course which favours horses that are nimble enough and possess sufficient stamina and adaptability to cope with its sharp bends and occasional quite sharp gradients.

In being so idiosyncratic, Plumpton is a track at which previous course winners should always receive close consideration.

Plumpton Racecourse
Plumpton
East Sussex BN7 3AL
Tel: (01273) 890383
www.plumptonracecourse.co.uk

HOW TO GET THERE:
From North: M23; A23; A272; A275
From South: A23; A273; B2112
From East: A27; A275
From West: A272; A275
By Rail: Plumpton
By Air: Helicopter facilities

PLUMPTON: Plan of the course.

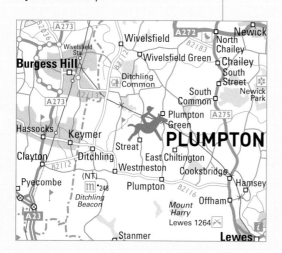

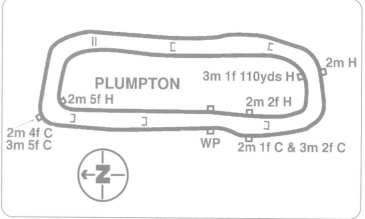

Pontefract

Long ago, such industrial landmarks as the slag heaps, collieries, a coking plant and a power station's chimneys could be seen from the grandstand at Pontefract. However, the vista looks far less industrial and much more attractive now and the proximity of this Yorkshire course to the major population centres of Bradford, Leeds and Sheffield (none of which is more than 25 miles away) ensures that it is well attended, as does it accessibility via motorways. If motorists leave the M62 at junction 32 they will soon find themselves on the track itself, while racegoers from the south will find the M1 part of a route that joins the M18 and A1. Rail travellers will find that Pontefract (Baghill) station can be reached via Sheffield, which itself lies on the main line from London St Pancras. Thereafter, they will need to take a short bus ride to the course.

Helicopters can land on the track by prior arrangement. Fixed-wing aircraft may be accommodated at Sherburn-in-Elmet, or alternatively at Yeadon.

Racing has long taken place at Pontefract, one of only five courses on which racing was allowed to continue in 1942 – a year when many felt it might well be discontinued, such were the difficulties being faced by the Allies at the time. In the 1960s Pontefract suffered mining subsidence that not only jeopardized the stability of the racecourse site, but also brought the water table so close to its subsoil that even a heavy shower made soft going something of a certainty. Fortunately, rubble obtained on the demolition of a local Methodist chapel greatly fortified the original shale and sand subsoil. To counteract ground that is too hard, the executive has also installed a modern watering system.

Pontefract, a pear-shaped oval extending for 2 miles 125 yards, is the longest flat racecourse in Great Britain. Its circuit reminds some racegoers of Brighton or Epsom. Pontefract, in fact, resembles both these courses in one further respect: it is an undulating affair that features a sharp turn or two.

The longest distance on which races are staged round Pontefract's switchback of a track is 2 miles 5 furlongs 122 yards, and the shortest 5 furlongs. In 6-furlong sprint events, the runners initially encounter level ground before it dips and begins to rise around the 4-furlong marker. Subsequently there is a gentle sweeping bend into the ascending 2-furlong run-in.

Since runners in every race at Pontefract are finally

Pontefract Racecourse
Park Lane
Pontefract
West Yorkshire WF8 4QL
Tel: (01977) 703224
www.pontefract-races.co.uk

HOW TO GET THERE:
From North: A1(M) (Junct. 42); M62 (Junct. 32)
From South: A1(M) (Junct. 42); M18; A1
From East: M62 (Junct. 32)
From West: M62 (Junct. 32)
By Rail: Baghill (bus to course)
By Air: Helicopter facilities

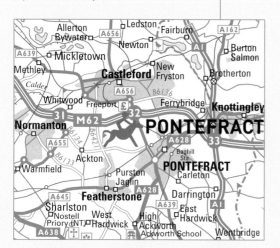

confronted by three punishing furlongs or so of rising ground, limitations in their stamina, courage and resolution will be ruthlessly exposed on this testing track.

In fact, Pontefract's sprint courses are generally regarded as some of the most severe in the country; thus the credentials of two-year-olds tackling them should be thoroughly scrutinized and their claims disregarded if they do not appear to be likely to stay or to relish a struggle. If you find a fast starter and a front runner with stamina that can grind down the opposition, then so much the better.

Horses tackling longer races of 2 miles 1 furlong 22 yards, 2 miles 1 furlong 216 yards and 2 miles 5 furlongs 122 yards have, once past the stands in the finishing straight, to race round a left-hand bend that runs downhill into a long back stretch that descends once the 12-furlong gate has been passed. Then come two left-handed dog leg turns (both fairly gradual) that lead to the shortest straight section of the track on the course, which extends from the starting point for 1 mile 4 yard races.

Next comes Pontefract's sharpest turn of all (almost 90 degrees), the penultimate one, which leads to the sprint course.

This wide, testing track features terrain that is so undulating that it is not really suitable for big, ungainly types which may find they are thrown out of their long strides.

At Pontefract, lowly drawn horses are favoured, above all in sprint races when the stalls are positioned on the far side. On soft going, this advantage increases even further. In races over 8 furlongs 4 yards and 10 furlongs 6 yards, which involve two left-hand bends, low-drawn contenders also have an edge.

Understandably, too, both horses and jockeys who have demonstrated mastery of this singular track enjoy an advantage.

Good viewing and much-improved facilities make this well-run track definitely worth a visit. It stages popular evening and Sunday meetings at which some racegoers patronize Pontefract's intriguingly named 'third' ring rather than the members', Tattersalls or the silver ring.

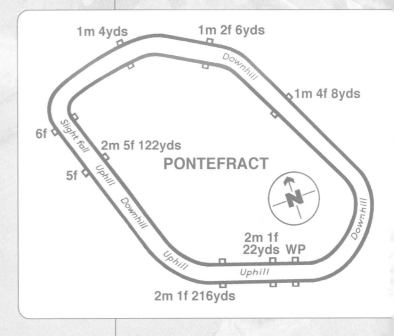

PONTEFRACT: Plan of the course.

Pontefract

Punchestown

Found in a most picturesque location, under three miles south-east of Naas and accessible from Newbridge railway station, Punchestown is one of Ireland's most distinctive, historic and prestigious racecourses. It is one of the places where Irish racing supporters love to congregate, dress stylishly and gamble fiercely.

The peerless National Hunt festival meeting held here in late April, when the gorse is in bloom, is unforgettable partly because this course is closer to open country than any other non-point-to-point track in England or Ireland.

Steeplechases at Punchestown take place on a right-handed undulating, rather rectangular-looking track that extends for 2 miles. With its sharp, almost 90-degree bend that horses negotiate on the fast circuit after passing the stands, its mixture of plain fences and open ditches, its downhill run and uphill climbs, its distinctive bank fence (a double affair) and its tricky final turn into a long run-in, it is no wonder that Punchestown is regarded as a taxing, but fair test of a 'lepper'. Indeed, when the going is heavy here it often pays to support a lightly weighted runner, especially in a longish race.

The hurdle track runs inside the 'chasing course for almost 1¾ miles, while flat races can also be staged over 6, 7½, 9 and 14 furlongs, on what is yet another testing track. On this, high numbers have a slight advantage.

Punchestown Racecourse
Naas
Co. Kildare
Ireland
Tel: 00 +353 (0)45 897704
www.punchestown.com

HOW TO GET THERE:
From North: R407; R411
From South: N18
From East: N7
From West: N7
By Rail: Newbridge
By Air: Dublin Airport

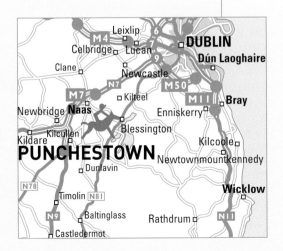

PUNCHESTOWN: Plan of the course.

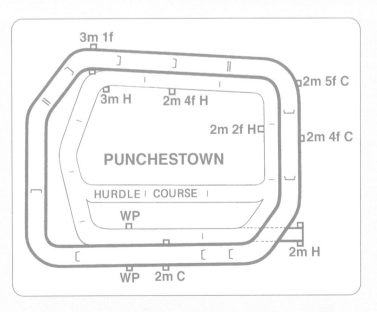

Punchestown

Of late, Punchestown's prestigious festival races have been the BMW Handicap Chase, the Champion Novice Hurdle, the Punchestown Heineken Gold Cup, Emo Oil Champion Hurdle and the Champion four-year-old hurdle, which has followed a most interesting spectacle – a 4-mile cross-country steeplechase which is run round a snaking obstacle course that includes a formidable double bank fence that is taken both ways.

Away from the festival, the Grand National Trial Handicap Chase is an important early-February Aintree rehearsal of 3 miles 2½ furlongs.

Such is the ambience at 'peerless' Punchestown, and so excellent the view and competitive the sport, that it is popular both with true enthusiasts and socialites. Punchestown is one racecourse on which few care if it rains or not.

In fact, only cancellation (as in 1950 when the April meeting was snowed off in apparent rebuke of the administrators who were erroneously celebrating the course's centenary) can keep the crowds away.

Redcar

Like Andy Capp, the cartoon character in the Daily Mirror, who gave his name to a race once staged on its left-handed surface, Redcar racecourse is unpretentiously distinctive. Its facilities rival many more fashionable courses and are available at very competitive prices.

What is so refreshing about Redcar, apart from its bracing location near Middlesbrough on the Yorkshire coast, to the north-east of some scenic moorland, is the fact that such facilities as private viewing and dining boxes are available to racegoers on a 'first come, first served' basis at very reasonable rates.

Well-equipped stands that afford an excellent view, many generously sponsored races, a paddock and a children's playground help to make racing at Redcar (where the Princess Royal once triumphed) an enjoyable experience. It is also likely to be a rather happy, carefree affair: the racecourse executive offers free admission to those under 16 and special discounts to parties that book in advance and many meetings take place during the holiday season.

Nor is there anything about this very fair Yorkshire track (apart from two sharp, semi-circular, left-hand bends that have to be negotiated in races of more than 1 mile) that is likely to bring any unhappiness to the horses that have to race over it.

Redcar Racecourse
Redcar, TS10 2BY
Tel: (01642) 484068
www.redcarracing.co.uk

HOW TO GET THERE:
From North: A1(M) (Junct. 57); A19; A174
From South: A1(M) (Junct. 57); A174
From East: A174 (from Whitby); A1085
By Rail: Redcar Central (from Darlington on East Coast line)
By Air: Teesside International Airport (tel: 01325 332811); Yearby

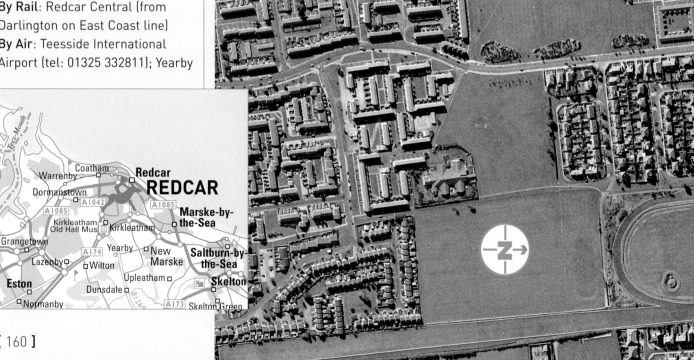

The course is long, narrow, practically flat, and oval, with a circumference of approaching 2 miles.

Highlights of Redcar's season include the Stanley Racing Zetland Gold Cup at the end of May, the valuable Two-Year-Old Trophy in early October, when a 'listed' race – the Guisborough Stakes – is also staged. Sunday fixtures in the summer attract large crowds while a popular 'Ladies' Night' on a Saturday in late August brings glamour to Redcar's only evening fixture.

Redcar's longest races are staged over 1 mile 6 furlongs 19 yards, and 2 miles and a few yards and thus are started some way short of the winning post.

After racing over a straight section of track, those involved have to negotiate a tight left-hand bend around which an inexperienced jockey may cause his mount to lose ground. Thereafter, Redcar's long back straight allows powerful galloping types to lengthen their strides and increase the pace. Then, after rounding a second 180-degree left-hand bend, those running in longer races enter a final straight run-in of 5 furlongs along which jockeys can ride a late finish as they tack over to the stands side. Making such a move as the straight course is joined seems very wise, as surveys have shown that of those contesting races of 8, 7, 6 or 5 furlongs, horses drawn high nearest the stands have an advantage, especially when the stalls are positioned on the stands side or in the centre of the track.

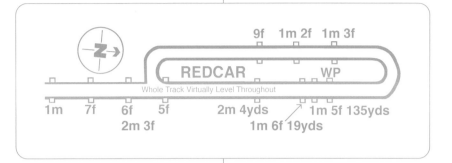

REDCAR: Plan of the course.

Ripon

Ripon, the 'garden racecourse', is to be found on meadowland between the river Ure and Ripon Canal in the Yorkshire Dales. It is not so sharp nor as narrow as Redcar and also differs from it in being right-handed.

The track itself, which is under two miles south-east of Ripon off the B6265 Boroughbridge Road, is some four miles from the Great North Road from the south (the A1(M)). The 200-mile train journey from London King's Cross terminates at Harrogate, some 11 miles away. Helicopters can land on-course and fixed-wing aircraft can be accommodated at Leeds/Bradford airport.

The course is a fairly tight oval of almost 14 furlongs. It presents thoroughbreds with a really fair test since its long wide straights are conducive to a good gallop.

A spur projecting from the round course provides a sprint track of 6 furlongs that has two distinguishing features whose extent or even existence have not always been acknowledged: a dip about a furlong out and relatively minor surface undulations throughout.

Ripon Racecourse
Boroughbridge Road
Ripon
North Yorkshire HG4 1UG
Tel: (01765) 602156
www.ripon-races.co.uk

HOW TO GET THERE:
From North: A1; A61; B6265
From South: A1(M); A61
From East: A170 (from Scarborough); A61
From West: A59 (from Preston); A61
By Rail: Harrogate (11 miles)
By Air: Helicopter facilities

The best-known sprint staged at Ripon is the great St Wilfrid Handicap which is run over 6 furlongs in August. Named after the patron saint of this cathedral city, it serves as a reminder of Ripon's ecclesiastical importance. A splendid silver trophy of St Wilfrid on horseback is presented to the winner.

The most prestigious race run on this course and one of only two that qualify for listed status is also over 6 furlongs. The Champion Two-Year-Old Trophy (which High Top, the 1972 2000 Guineas winner, captured prior to his triumph at Newmarket) is one of the main attractions of the holiday meeting that is held on the last Monday in August.

In general, Ripon's sprint track favours fast starters and front-running types that can steal a march over their rivals on its wide straight.

A glance at the photograph suggests that the bends on this round course are tight and likely to be appreciated by handy, well-balanced animals. However, the photograph does not reveal the banking that has made their negotiation a little easier in recent seasons. Despite this, some long-striding types lose their balance round the last bend.

RIPON: Plan of the course.

Salisbury

Salisbury Racecourse
Netherhampton
Salisbury
Wiltshire SP2 8PN
Tel: (01722) 326461
www.salisburyracecourse.co.uk

HOW TO GET THERE:

From North: A345; A338

From South: A338 (from Ringwood); A354 (from Blandford Forum)

From East: M3 (Junct. 8); A303; A360 (to Wilton)

From West: M4 (Junct. 15); A346; A338

By Rail: Salisbury (3½ miles)

By Air: Helicopter facilities

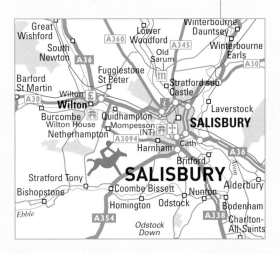

Salisbury's downland course is held in high regard, not just with local handlers operating from several training centres in the area (Marlborough and Devizes to name but two), but also by trainers from much further afield. This is because, in being so testing and yet quite fairly so, Salisbury allows trainers to introduce promising newcomers to racing and to assess their potential.

This particular ploy was demonstrated to perfection as long ago as 1912 when Aboyeur, the eventual 100–1 winner of the Derby of the following year, made a winning debut in an important two-year-old race, the 6-furlong Champagne Stakes. Fifty-eight years later, Mill Reef, after making an impressive winning debut at Salisbury, went on in his second season to capture the Derby in 1971, and so underline the lesson.

Historically then, Salisbury has attracted horses of the highest class. One of these was the legendary Eclipse, winner of all the 26 races and matches in which he took part before his death in 1789. Interestingly, one of these victories was in the City Bowl Handicap Stakes, a race now replaced by a fillies handicap, contested in June.

Another historical and prestigious Salisbury race is the Bibury Cup, a 12-furlong handicap for three-year-olds that is staged in late June as part of a two-day fixture which is still known as the 'Bibury Meeting'.

A 6-furlong handicap run in early July, recalls Fred Darling's Owen Tudor. Other famous horses commemorated by Salisbury races are the speedy Myrobella, with a 5-furlong sprint for two-year-olds in July, and Fair Trial, remembered by a mile handicap for three-year-olds run at the same fixture. Five listed races are now seen at Salisbury – the most valuable of which is the 1-mile Sovereign Stakes that is contested in mid-August.

Developing types running at Salisbury will often reveal whether they have sufficient courage, stamina and resolution to compete successfully in the highest class. Moreover, if horses that can hold their own on top-class courses, have a run at Salisbury while still not fully fit, they are likely to do themselves full justice when they subsequently step up in class.

Large numbers of horses compete at Salisbury's fairly frequent meetings. Indeed, on Thursday 11 September 1980 the Marlborough Stakes for two-year-old maidens attracted no less than 62 runners and thus had to be divided into four divisions.

The course proves popular thanks to its conformation which makes considerable, but not Draconian, demands on racehorses in every race in which rising ground is encountered.

Runners over 1 mile 6 furlongs and 15 yards, the longest distance on this rather punishing track, run the 'wrong way' to the winning post that is not far away. Then it's downhill past the 12-furlong start and soon afterwards they swing left to enter a sharp right-hand loop which initially involves the start of a 'short' 10 furlongs and a straight stretch of still-descending ground. Then comes an extremely tight, semi-circular, right-handed bend that rises as, about 6½ furlongs from home, the loop runs into the so-called 'straight' course which, in fact, features a right-handed elbow. Thanks to a spur, the straight course extends for a mile, of which most of the first 2 furlongs is uphill. Then a fairly flat section of track continues for a furlong until, thereafter, the ground rises steadily for the final 4 furlongs, so that by the post the runners are 76 feet higher than at the start of the course. Salisbury's largely uphill straight course calls for resolution in those who tackle it. Apart from possessing stamina and courage, horses running on the round course need to be sufficiently handy and adaptable to cope with its camber and its very sharp and semi-circular, top right-hand bend. Jockeys need the skill both to tack over gradually to the inside running rail on entering the loop and go the shortest way round the final turn, and to also help their mounts keep something in reserve for the rather punishing closing stages of their races.

Racing over 5 and 6 furlongs, 6 furlongs 212 yards and 1 mile is, if anything, an even more taxing experience than running in longer races because, for those concerned, most of the ground, especially in the closing stages, rises relentlessly to the line.

As for the draw at Salisbury, in races up to a mile, this favours the lowly drawn if the stalls are on the stands side or in the centre, but high-drawn horses have the edge if the stalls are on the far side.

Soft ground is sometimes found at Salisbury, whose subsoil is downland chalk. This, however, supports a deep layer of luxuriant

SALISBURY: Plan of the course.

Salisbury

and resilient spring turf which makes for an unrivalled racing surface. Jockeys bring the horses up the stands rail when the ground is soft.

Salisbury is one of England's oldest racecourses (a meeting was held here in 1584) and is a most civilized track that is strictly managed, picturesquely situated, and offers a scenic view of Salisbury Cathedral.

Buses are on hand at Salisbury station (which is just over 80 miles

from London's Waterloo), to take rail travellers a further 3½ miles westwards to the course. Motorists will find this lies off the A3094 road to Netherhampton. The track is, in fact, situated 23 miles from Southampton and 30 miles from Bournemouth, and offers free car parking facilities. Those who wish to travel in style can make use of a helicopter landing pad, unlike Queen Elizabeth I who, apparently, took in a Salisbury meeting before seeing off Drake's task force against the Armada.

Sandown Park

Sandown Park Racecourse
Esher
Surrey KT10 9AJ
Tel: (01372) 463072
www.sandown.co.uk

HOW TO GET THERE:

From North: M1 (Junct. 6A); M25 (Junct. 10); A224

From South: A3; M25 (Junct. 10); A224

From East: M25 (Junct. 10); A224

From West: M3 (Junct. 2); M25 (Junct. 10); A224

By Rail: Esher

By Air: Fairoaks airstrip; Helicopter facilities

Those who regularly patronize this attractive track enjoy a veritable feast of first-class sport. Indeed, the racing fare they are offered in the course of a season is extremely varied and is made up of some rather exotic ingredients.

One has a distinctive Chinese flavour in featuring the Royal Hong Kong Jockey Club Handicap, while a colourful Harpers and Queen evening meeting has included a Green Welly Claiming Stakes when staged in July.

It should not, however, be concluded that racing at Sandown is bizarre. This, after all, is the course on which the Eclipse Stakes (England's first £10,000 race whose inaugural running took place in 1886) is staged in honour of the Darley Arabian's great-great-grandson who established himself as the greatest race horse of the eighteenth century.

Sandown's spring meeting, on the last Saturday in April, boasts the 10 furlong 7 yard Classic Trial which can provide useful pointers to the Classic chances of the top-class three-year-old colts and geldings that contest it as part of their Derby preparation. The winner of this race will often be in a high position in the ante-post betting lists for the colts' Classic. Run over the same course and distance is the Gordon Richards Stakes, which is limited to more mature horses. Another top race run at the late April meeting is the Sandown Mile.

A later two-day Sandown fixture (towards the end of May) includes the 5 furlong 6 yard Temple Stakes, in which three-year-olds have often defeated their older rivals. Also run at this meeting are the historic 2 mile 78 yard Henry II Stakes for four-year-olds and above and the Brigadier Gerard Stakes, which commemorates John Hislop's celebrated winner of the Eclipse Stakes over course and distance of 10 furlongs and 7 yards.

As for the Eclipse Stakes, which brings together the very best middle-distance three-year-olds and their seniors in intriguing rivalry over the above distance, it is run on the first Saturday in July so that Classic contenders at Epsom have had time to prepare for it. Past victories have been divided fairly equally between three- and four-year-olds. Quite regularly the Eclipse is won by a Classic winner.

The Solario Stakes is an important 7 furlong 16 yard contest for two-year-olds that takes place at Sandown in late August. It commemorates a colt whose victories during 1925 and 1926 in the St Leger, Coronation Cup and

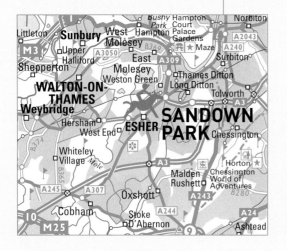

Ascot Gold Cup were over rather longer distances.

Sandown nestles in a natural amphitheatre and offers an excellent view of the racing, which seems particularly spectacular largely because its oval circuit extends away from the stands and so is clearly and completely visible from them.

The flat course is an oval affair that extends for about 13 furlongs on which the longest races (like the Henry II Stakes) are staged over 2 miles 78 yards. Those involved in such contests start in the finishing straight 3 furlongs or so from the post, and thus have to initially contend with the majority of the course's rather stiff, 4-furlong run-in that only levels out about 50 yards from the finish. Horses tackling not only 2 miles, but also 14 furlongs, at Sandown, encounter some undulating terrain after the winning post has been passed and they negotiate a reasonably sweeping right-hand bend. This leads to a downhill straight section of track which precedes a sharper right-hand bend that falls as it turns to join Sandown's largely level back straight. This course section (which has two spurs projecting from it to allow races over 10 furlongs 7 yards and 1 mile 14 yards to be staged) is fairly flat.

It is when they have negotiated the track's final, fairly sharp and semi-circular, right-hand bend that for around 4½ furlongs all Sandown finishers are confronted with rising ground. As is to be expected of those running this right-handed round course, the highly drawn are favoured.

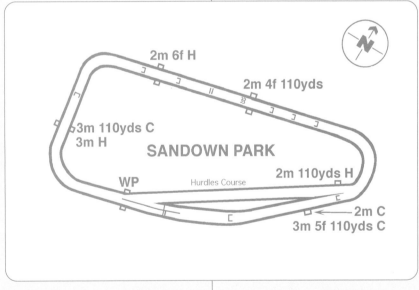

SANDOWN PARK: Plans of the Flat course (top) and the National Hunt course (bottom).

Sandown also has a separate straight course on which, unusually, no 6-furlong races can be contested since it only extends for a little over 5 furlongs. However, to compensate for lack of length it rises steadily throughout its 5 furlongs. Thus, it is worth checking to see if one's selection, particularly if it is a two-year-old, has stamina on its side.

As for the draw, it has been estimated that at Sandown, if a sprint is run on soft going and the stalls are placed on the far side, high-drawn horses have as much as a 1 lb advantage per stall, which is significant since 10 lbs can be considered as equivalent to an 'edge' of over three lengths.

Jockeys must appreciate the danger of prematurely easing their mounts on both the hilly section of the run-in and its final flat 50 yards and shouldn't leave them too much ground to make up in the taxing final stages of their races.

Generally, Sandown favours dour, long-striding, galloping types whose strong point is stamina, while it tends to expose the limitations of irresolute animals that are unlikely to stay. It does not really suit front runners, yet is not too severe a test for the stout-hearted.

Since it stands on soil that drains well, the going during the flat season is seldom heavy.

As for steeplechasing, Sandown is, in the view of many, the pre-eminent park racecourse. Indeed, for many the jumping year only really starts with the New Year running of the Mildmay Cazalet Memorial Handicap Chase, which recalls the Queen Mother's former trainer, Peter Cazalet, and the late Lord Mildmay. This 29½ furlong race provides a Grand National pointer and is frequently won by an eight-year-old.

The Imperial Cup is a handicap hurdle that is a 'curtain raiser' to the Cheltenham Festival when it is staged on the first or second Saturday in March.

Sandwiched into Sandown's 'mixed' late April meeting is the At The Races Gold Cup, which is run over 3 miles 5½ furlongs and often produces some thrilling finishes as when Special Cargo narrowly prevailed in 1984. Some high-class horses have won this splendid spectacle including Pas Seul, Arkle, Mill House, The Dikler, Diamond Edge and Desert Orchid. Nine-year-olds often go well on the firmer ground that this race frequently involves. Such conditions rarely feature in the William Hill Handicap Hurdle in late November or early December. This race is always a fairly competitive affair and can involve some heavy betting.

Sandown's compact jumping track is a right-handed oval of around 13 furlongs which finally involves a taxing uphill run after the last bend has been rounded. Its 11 fences, especially the three so-called 'railway' fences that come in such quick succession in the back straight, represent a severe test of a horse's jumping ability. The first fence that three-milers take is downhill; then in the back stretch come two plain fences that are followed by an open ditch. Next comes the water jump and then the three plain 'railway' fences. The plain 'pond' fence is part of the bend into the straight in which there are two final obstacles. The first is a plain fence, while the second is a 'split', in that on the first circuit an open ditch is involved, but on the final lap the runners take a plain fence which is followed by an uphill run to the line of 300 yards. All hurdle races are run on the flat course.

Few today would regard a day out at Sandown as dauntingly expensive. While a few might see its splendid facilities (which include banqueting suites) as the trappings of privilege, refreshingly all the facilities on-course are available on a 'first come, first served' basis and lady racegoers are made to feel particularly welcome.

This attractive, meticulously managed, course lies five miles from Kingston upon Thames and 14 miles from Guildford. It is adjacent to Esher station which can be reached rapidly and conveniently from London's Waterloo some 15 miles away.

A playground in the park enclosure caters for children and, for adults, generous reduced rates of admission are offered to parties of more than 100 racegoers, a concession quite frequently granted.

If there is a slight shortcoming at Sandown it is the course's failure to present thoroughbreds with an opportunity to race over the full Derby distance. However, this is a minor deficiency.

Sandown Park

Sandown Park

Sedgefield

Sedgefield Racecourse
Sedgefield
Stockton-on-Tees TS21 2HW
Tel: (01740) 621925
www.sedgefield-
racecourse.co.uk

HOW TO GET THERE:

From North: A1(M) (Junct. 60);
A689

From South: A1(M) (Junct. 60);
A19 (from Thirsk)

From East: A689

From West: A689 (from Bishop
Auckland)

By Rail: Stockton-on-Tees
(5 miles); Darlington (8 miles)

By Air: Teesside International
Airport; Middlesbrough

On this left-handed, undulating track there are eight fairly easy, well-made obstacles. Despite the fact that Sedgefield means 'Cedd's open land', its racecourse only extends for 10 furlongs and is a sharp affair. Its fences are quite closely positioned; thus a run on this track calls for both jumping ability and adaptability.

It also puts the stamina of those (especially steeplechasers) who run on it fully on trial, since from the second last there is a steep downhill run that is followed by a punishing final uphill stretch which extends for over 500 yards, the water jump being omitted on the final circuit. Thus, when the going is heavy here one needs to side with a dour stayer.

On the hurdle course the run-in from the last obstacle is only 200 yards.

The viewing at Sedgefield is excellent and often horses can be seen in spectacular action and silhouetted against the winter skyline.

The fact that so many days' racing are staged at Sedgefield – most of them on Tuesdays – testifies to its popularity. This is partly due to its proximity to the towns of Middlesbrough, Darlington and Durham. The track itself, which offers splendid viewing, is to be found in a peaceful rural location. Indeed, its remoteness deters some rail travellers who have to take quite an extensive taxi ride to the course, from either Stockton or Darlington station.

The course is just off the A1(M) and is conveniently reached via the A689. Those travelling north-west from Middlesbrough should take the A177, join the A689 and look for signs directing them to the course, which is to the south-west of Sedgefield itself. Those coming westwards from Bishop Auckland can remain on the A689.

Helicopters can be accommodated on-course. These and fixed-wing aircraft can, however, land at Teesside International Airport from which taxis can be taken.

The McEwans National is an often-thrilling, long-distance handicap steeplechase that is staged at Sedgefield in early March. Confined to five-year-olds and above, this is a 3½-mile contest.

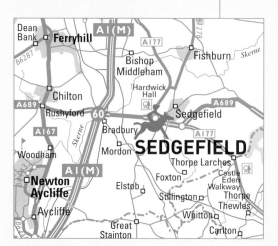

SEDGEFIELD: Plan of the course.

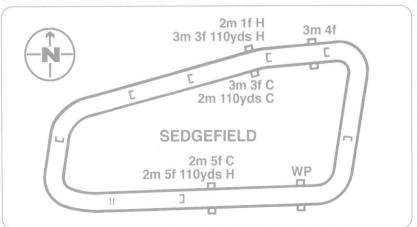

2m 1f H
3m 3f 110yds H
3m 4f
3m 3f C
2m 110yds C
SEDGEFIELD
2m 5f C
2m 5f 110yds H
WP

Southwell

Formerly operating merely as a National Hunt course, Southwell has come into further prominence of late as a venue for all-weather racing.

A race track has long been sited at Rolleston, north-east of Nottingham and some three miles from Southwell, where the jumping circuit is a 10-furlong, oval, left-hander with tight bends and reasonably easy fences. However, since these are unevenly spaced – two in the long back stretch are close together just before the sharp final turn into the short 250-yard run-in – they can present difficulties to long-striding gallopers.

Speedy, adaptable runners do well on this sharp course on which the viewing is perfectly adequate.

Nottingham can be reached from London St Pancras by rail and a bus service connects the city to the Rolleston track. This scenic course is four miles west of Newark and can be conveniently reached by many on the A617. Junction 25 is the one to make for if travelling on the M1.

The all-weather Fibresand course is 10 furlongs in extent and features a 3-furlong run-in. Flat and hurdle races are run on the same course. A 5-furlong course is provided by a spur while the 6-furlong track takes in two semi-circular bends.

Fibresand, now a well-tried, all-weather racing surface, tends to be fairly taxing to race over, so it is worth checking to see whether one's selection at Southwell has stamina on its side.

Southwell Racecourse
Rolleston
Newark
Nottinghamshire NG25 0TS
Tel: 0870 220 2332
www.southwell-racecourse.co.uk

HOW TO GET THERE:
From North: A1 (to Newark); A617; M1 (Junct. 25); A52; A46
From South: M1 (Junct. 25); A52 (to Nottingham); A46
From East: A17 (from Sleaford, Boston)
From West: A617 (from Mansfield)
By Rail: Rolleston
By Air: Tollerton Aerodrome; Helicopter facilities

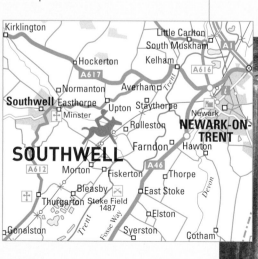

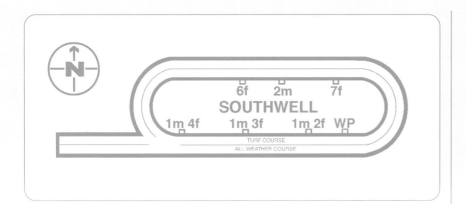

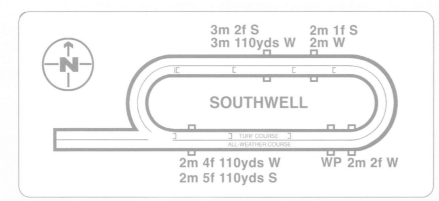

SOUTHWELL: Plan of the Flat (turf and all-weather) course (top) and the National Hunt (turf and all-weather) course (bottom).

Stratford-on-Avon

With its view of the bard's resting place at Holy Trinity and some pleasant countryside, Stratford-on-Avon's racecourse is an agreeable place to spend an evening or afternoon. It is well managed and is popular with racing professionals and parties of racegoers, a fair number of whom speak with Welsh accents!

The track itself is a fairly triangular, tight left-hander that extends for over 1¼ miles. It is largely flat except in parts of its back straight. The fences, which sadly no longer include a water jump, are in front of the stands and are not terribly testing.

There are two fences in the home straight and since the run-in is only 200 yards, horses need to be handily placed as they round the final well-banked, rather sweeping turn which is far less tight than the top bend. The latter is close to the 2 mile 1½ furlong and 3 mile 4 furlong starts.

The course lies a mile outside Stratford off the B439 Evesham road. The A46 is an ideal route from north or south: motorists from the latter direction will find this connects with a recently completed stretch of the M40. The A422 is a useful route for those arriving in Stratford from the west.

The opposite bookend to Stratford's significant Saturday meeting in October is the Saturday in early June when the Champion Intrum Justitia Hunters' Chase, staged in front of a large crowd, effectively closes the 'main' jumping season.

Another important hunter 'chase is staged at a Friday evening meeting prior to Intrum Justitia day in June (which actually features a parade by huntsmen and the Warwickshire pack of foxhounds); this is the John Corbet Cup. Other races have recalled Garrick, the Shakespearean actor, and several are now run, thanks to watering from the Avon, in late June, July and August.

Stratford is memorable for its competitive racing, sporting atmosphere and an excellent view of the action, even from the cheapest enclosure.

Stratford-on-Avon Racecourse
Luddington Road
Stratford-on-Avon
Warwickshire CV37 9SE
Tel: (01789) 267949
www.stratfordracecourse.net

HOW TO GET THERE:
From North: M42; M40 (Junct. 15); A46
From South: M40 (Junct. 15); A46; M5 (Junct. 7); A44; A46; B439
From East: A422 (from Banbury)
From West: A422 (from Worcester)
By Rail: Stratford-on-Avon
By Air: Helicopter facilities

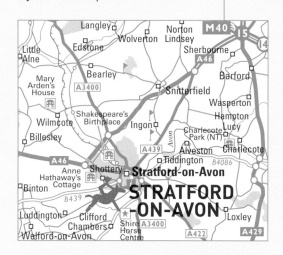

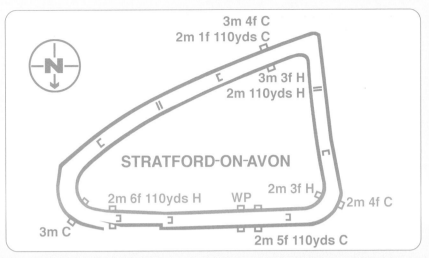

3m 4f C
2m 1f 110yds C

3m 3f H
2m 110yds H

STRATFORD-ON-AVON

2m 6f 110yds H   WP   2m 3f H

2m 4f C

3m C

2m 5f 110yds C

STRATFORD-ON-AVON:
Plan of the course

Taunton

Taunton is very much a country racecourse which affords fine views of the Blackdown Hills to the south and the Quantocks to the north. It lies more than two miles south of the town from which it takes its name.

It is a long, oval-shaped, right-handed course of 10 furlongs in extent which, in essence, consists of two long straights and two rather tight, but still reasonably easy, semi-circular bends. There are seven unformidable fences on what is rather misleadingly called Taunton's 'circuit' whose most taxing feature is a final 3-furlong stretch of rising ground.

The short 150-yard run-in is encountered once the final three fences in the finishing straight (which are visible from the stands) have been negotiated.

Past course winners should be supported on this rather singular racecourse.

Of notable races staged at Taunton, two are memorials commemorating Gay Sheppard and John Thorne while, interestingly, a Hangover Selling Hurdle has also been contested.

This informal, friendly racecourse (on which pleasant picnics can be taken in its central enclosure) is readily accessible since it is close to junction 25 of the M5. Those arriving by road will find that the track is quietly, even sleepily, situated south of Taunton off the B3170.

Rail travellers need to depart from London Paddington for Taunton station and thence take a taxi-ride of approximately three and a half miles to Orchard Portman itself, or rather the estate of this name on which, in 1927, the track was laid out by the fifth Viscount Portman.

Air travellers should note that, with prior permission, helicopters can land on Taunton's runway.

However they arrive, racegoers will find themselves in a picturesque setting among some genial jumping enthusiasts.

TAUNTON: Plan of the course.

Taunton Racecourse
Orchard Portman
Taunton
Somerset TA3 7BL
Tel: (01823) 337172
www.tauntonracecourse.co.uk

HOW TO GET THERE:
From North: M5 (Junct. 25)
From South: M5 (Junct. 25); A30 (from Honiton); B3170
From East: A303 (to Ilminster); A358
From West: A361 (from Barnstaple); M5 (Junct. 25)
By Rail: Taunton
By Air: Helicopter facilities

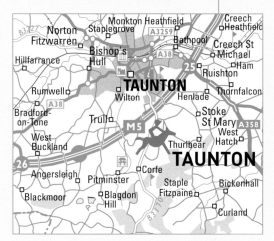

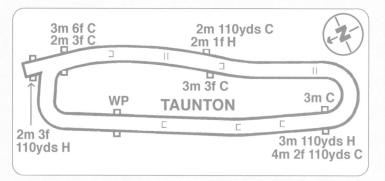

Thirsk

Thirsk Racecourse
Station Road
Thirsk
North Yorkshire YO7 1QL
Tel: (01845) 522276
www.thirskracecourse.net

HOW TO GET THERE:
From North: A1; A61; A19; A61
From South: A1; A61; A19; A61
From East: A170 (from Pickering, Scarborough)
From West: A61 (from Ripon)
By Rail: Thirsk (half a mile from course)
By Air: Helicopter facilities

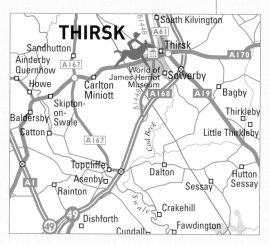

Thirsk's extremely scenic racecourse still has a link with high-class racing through a Classic trial (a Guineas rehearsal) staged in early April on the fine old grassland of this extremely pleasant track.

This particular race is keenly contested. From its inception in 1948, it attracted high-class horses and was won in its time by Alycidon, Nimbus (the 1949 2000 Guineas and Derby winner), Sweet Solera (victorious in both the 1000 Guineas and the Oaks), and more recently, by High Top (winner of the first of the colts' Classics of the 1972 season).

An even more historic race is the Hambleton Cup Handicap, a 12-furlong affair that is contested in early September.

This event, which was staged before racing commenced on its present site in 1855 and was formerly a 2-mile Cesarewitch trial, is a reminder to racegoers that Northern racing folk used to hold meetings at what was once their 'headquarters' at Hambleton. Noteworthy too is the perhaps better-known Thirsk Hunt Cup, a fairly valuable mile handicap contested in early May.

In fact, racing does not take place all that frequently on this fairly flat, quite sharp, left-handed oval track which has rather a small circumference of 10 furlongs or so. The bends at Thirsk are not as difficult to negotiate as a glance at the Ordnance Survey map might suggest; nonetheless, speedy, adaptable types relish a run on this track on which long-striding animals or awkward runners can sometimes fail to settle.

Thirsk is a very fair track, popular with both trainers and jockeys and some of its races are contested by sizeable fields which often include one or two 'raiders' from southern stables.

The turf at Thirsk provides a good racing surface on which the going is seldom extreme. An irrigation system ensures that firm ground, which once caused fields to cut up fairly appreciably during dry spells, is now more rare.

As for the course, it is a straightforward affair that in appearance is rather reminiscent of a paper clip. Basically, the straight sprint course of 6 furlongs, which also allows races to be staged over the minimum distance, is rather more undulating than the final straight of the round course into which it runs just under 4 furlongs out.

In the large fields that frequently line up for sprint races, those drawn high seem to have an edge when the stalls are on the stands side (where the runners tend to converge), an advantage increased on soft ground, as a better surface only involves a narrow strip near the stands rail.

Horses tackling 2 miles at Thirsk also travel along the straight spur that allows sprints to be staged. On joining the round course after just over 2 furlongs, they encounter ground which features undulations that are even more gradual than any they have already negotiated on the spur. Just before the final stages of the run-in, prior to passing the finishing post for the first time, the runners pass the point from which races over 12 furlongs are started. The rest of the round course is virtually flat and initially takes them round the first of Thirsk's bends which is more gradual and less sharp and semi-circular than its successor.

Thirsk's back straight, along which races over 8 furlongs and just under7 furlongs are started, extends for approximately 3 furlongs. Finally, once a fairly tight final bend has been rounded, all that remains is the run-in of just under 4 furlongs which undulates along its complete length.

The railway station, a half a mile walk away from the track, lies on the main line from King's Cross. Station Road is one mile to the west of Thirsk which can be reached via the A61 from Ripon or the A170 from Pickering and Scarborough. Those arriving from the south will find that Thirsk lies six miles east of the A1. From York the A19 should be taken.

Despite the fact that it is not particularly close to large-population centres, Thirsk is well attended and often patronized by southern professionals, even though it is over 210 miles from the capital. Some of these individuals arrive in helicopters that can land on the course's hockey pitch, while those in fixed-wing aircraft may be able to land at Allanbrooke Barracks at Topcliffe, close to Thirsk.

Of late, much has been spent on course improvements, including new stands in the enclosures.

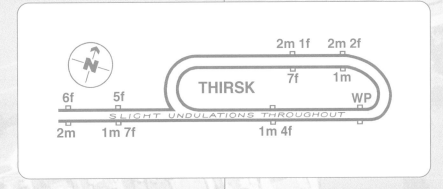

THIRSK: Plan of the course.

Thirsk

Thirsk

Towcester

The truly rural and Corinthian flavour of racing at Towcester is certainly suggested by the fact that one of its principal races has been the Empress of Austria Hunters' Chase, the highlight of a spring meeting.

The racecourse was originally laid out on a picturesque Northamptonshire country estate.

The course is square and extends for approaching a mile and three-quarters. Even though its back stretch is downhill, the circuit ends in an uphill 6-furlong slog which is understandably very punishing to race over when rain makes the clay racing surface extremely sticky. Thus many front runners tire and are overhauled on the 200-yard or so run-in.

In the summer firm ground can prevail and this is one further reason for checking that one's selection is a stayer and a good enough jumper not to be unsettled by two tricky fences in the downhill back stretch.

One of the charms of this track is the fine view one can obtain of horses running over the stamina-sapping ten-fence circuit that, for good measure, is a right-hander.

Towcester Racecourse
Easton Neston
Towcester
Northants NN12 7HS
Tel: (01327) 353414
www.towcester-racecourse.co.uk

HOW TO GET THERE:
From North: M1 (Junct. 15A); A5
From South: M1 (Junct. 15A); M40 (Junct. 10); A43; A5
From East: A45; A43; A5
From West: M40 (Junct. 11); A422; A43; A5
By Rail: Northampton (9 miles); Milton Keynes (11 miles)
By Air: Helicopter facilities

TOWCESTER: Plan of the course.

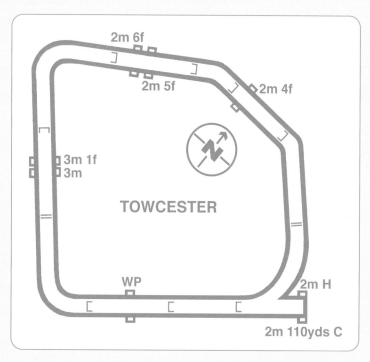

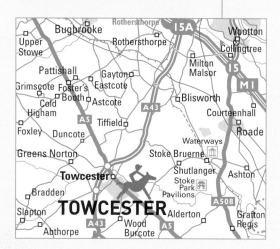

The track is nine miles south-west of Northampton and lies one mile south-east of the town from which it takes its name. It can be conveniently approached via the A43 which can be reached from the M40. The M1 runs nearby; leave at junction 15A if coming from the south, or travelling from the north.

Taxis run from Milton Keynes, which is 11 miles away, and Northampton, nine miles away – whose stations can be reached from Euston. Helicopters can be accommodated on-course. Lying only 60 miles from London, Towcester attracts good crowds. Some of its fixtures coincide with public holidays, including a two-day Easter meeting featuring the Schilizzi series of races.

Towcester

Tralee

Tralee dominates Irish horseracing for a week in late August/early September. Ever since the Rose of Tralee Festival was inaugurated in 1969, with the Directors of Tralee Races the prime movers, the Rose Festival and the Tralee Races have complemented each other.

With the first day of the Race Meeting coinciding with the final day of the Rose Festival, the craic and excitement at the racecourse on the Tuesday is rivalled by the unforgettable experience of a night in the town with the selection of the new Rose and a host of free street entertainment. This Festive atmosphere permeates the entire five days of the race meeting, making it for the punter and non-punter alike a most memorable and enjoyable occasion.

One of the highlights for the new Rose in her official capacity is to visit the races on the Wednesday with her fellow Roses. Two great Festivals come together as the Roses bring glamour and style to the day as they mingle with Racegoers. Great excitement is created as the new Rose is driven in an open carriage past the packed stands to the enclosure. The Rose is introduced to the crowd and presents the trophies to the winning connections after the Rose of Tralee Race.

Major races run during the five-day fixture include the Guinness Gold Cup Handicap, the Patsy Byrne Handicap Hurdle, the Tralee Handicap Chase, the Rose of Tralee Ladies' Race (which has had Indian, American and French, as well as Irish and English winners), the Denny Gold Medal Handicap Chase, the Carlsberg Ruby Stakes and the Brandon Hotel Handicap Hurdle.

The 9-furlong track is sharpish, undulating and essentially circular with six obstacles. The steeplechase course runs inside the flat and hurdle course and its final feature is a taxing steep uphill climb to the finish. Tralee is a course which makes considerable demands on the stamina of those who run on it, especially when the ground is soft, as it can be, even during August.

The racecourse is only half a mile from Tralee station, while air travellers can be accommodated, if appropriate, on a 200-metre on-course airstrip, if they are previously granted permission. Farranfore regional airport is 16 miles away.

Motorists coming from Cork should take the N22 north-westwards, from Dublin the N7 westwards towards Limerick, and from there the N21 or the N69 coastal route via Tarbert.

Tralee Racecourse
Ballybeggan Park
Tralee
Co. Kerry
Ireland
Tel: +353 (0)66 7126490

HOW TO GET THERE:
From North: N69
From South: N70
From East: N21
From West: R558; R560
By Rail: Tralee
By Air: Light Aircraft facilities; Farranfore Airport

TRALEE: plan of the course.

Uttoxeter

Staffordshire contains some good hunting country and it is thus appropriate that the Midlands' National takes place at Uttoxeter, which is to be found in this county close to the Peak District.

The track will be found in a pleasantly rural location and adjoins Uttoxeter railway station, itself accessible by train from St Pancras if one completes a 135-mile journey by changing at Derby.

Given its central location in being 16 miles from Burton-on-Trent, Uttoxeter draws crowds from all points of the compass.

Many motorists take the M6, leave at junction 15 and then continue on the ring road. The track will be found east of Stafford from which it is best approached via the A518. Helicopters can be accommodated on the course.

The track, a spectator's delight, is an essentially oval left-hander of around 11 furlongs with a flat home straight and a short run-in of around 170 yards from the last fence.

The Midlands' National is run over 4 miles 2 furlongs on some undulating terrain (there is a 1-furlong uphill stretch in the back straight and a short slight fall round the final bend); Uttoxeter's fairly easy bends and fences (the three most demanding of which are all in the home stretch) mean that front runners are favoured, as are speedy gallopers.

As well as its often-thrilling Aintree rehearsal, the March fixture also features another prestigious race, the Bet with the Tote Novices' Handicap Chase.

Another prestigious race staged at Uttoxeter is the Staffordshire Hurdle that is sufficiently important to be included in some diary lists of principal races contested each season. This is staged early in May.

Uttoxeter is deservedly popular both with racegoers who appreciate such amenities as modern grandstands, betting hall, bars and restaurants, and with their children who can find funfairs on hand to entertain them.

Uttoxeter Racecourse
Wood Lane
Uttoxeter
Staffs ST14 8BD
Tel: (01889) 562561
www.uttoxeter-racecourse.co.uk

HOW TO GET THERE:
From North: M6 (Junct. 15); A50
From South: M6 (Junct. 14); A513; A518
From East: A50
From West: A50; A518 (from Stafford)
By Rail: Uttoxeter (adjoins course)
By Air: Helicopter facilities

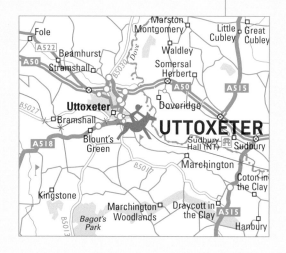

UTTOXETER: Plan of the
course.

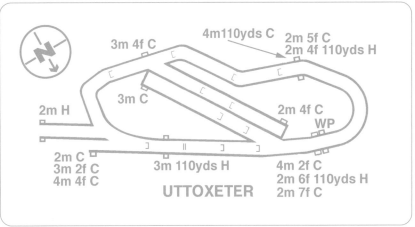

3m 4f C   4m110yds C   2m 5f C
                           2m 4f 110yds H

N

3m C

2m H   2m 4f C

                                   WP

2m C   3m 110yds H   4m 2f C
3m 2f C   2m 6f 110yds H
4m 4f C   **UTTOXETER**   2m 7f C

Warwick

Warwick Racecourse
Hampton Street
Warwick CV34 6HN
Tel: (01926) 491553
www.warwickracecourse.co.uk

HOW TO GET THERE:

From North: M6 (Junct. 4); M42; M40 (Junct. 15); A46

From South: M40 (Junct. 15); A46

From East: A45 (from Northampton); A425

From West: M42; M40; A422; A46

By Rail: Warwick, Leamington (3 miles)

By Air: Birmingham Airport

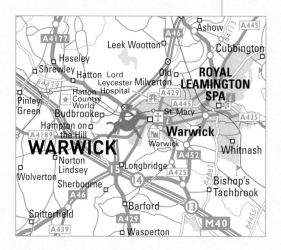

One of the oldest racecourses in the country is to be found at Warwick, close to the centre of this attractive country town.

By the early nineteenth century racing was well established here and was certainly more prestigious then than is the case today. However, despite the fact that the sporting fare on offer here is hardly top-class, it is pleasantly palatable which seems appropriate in that, historically, so many of its ingredients, like the Brooke Bond Oxo Man Appeal Stakes, have had connections with food!

The track itself, often misleadingly described as almost circular, is a broad, round-edged, quadrilateral-like affair which extends for over 1 mile and 5 furlongs. The longest flat races at Warwick are not staged over this distance but in excess of 2¼ miles. Those concerned start from the 5-furlong start on the spur that allows sprints to be staged and, after negotiating a left-handed dog leg past the winning post, then negotiate the least sharp of Warwick's four turns. Passing the one and a half mile start, they encounter steeply rising ground into the next straight track section as they round a fairly tight bend (from which a spur projects to provide an opportunity for horses to run over a distance approaching 1 mile 3 furlongs).

Thus, those involved in such events initially race up an incline before descending ground is encountered. The turn into the far straight is tight and from it a second spur projects to allow races to be held over 1 mile. Also started from points along this back straight (which is the longest straight section of the course) are events over 7 and 6 furlongs.

Warwick's short run-in extends for not much more than 2 furlongs. It also forms the final stage of a 5-furlong sprint course that is initially provided by a longish spur which projects at a fairly sharp, around 30-degree, angle from the final bend. The most pronounced feature of the sprint track is the elbow it begins to describe just before it joins the circuit.

If anything, advantage in the draw for races over 5 furlongs lies with those allotted high numbers. For races over Warwicks 'short' courses of 11 and 13 furlongs, low-drawn runners enjoy a slight edge.

Since much of the course has a clay subsoil, there is occasionally some give in its ground.

The Warwick Oaks, run over a distance longer than its Epsom equivalent in mid- or late-June, is typical of races here in not being particularly prestigious. Some, like the Kingmaker Handicap and the Anne Hathaway Stakes, have served as reminders of Warwick's historical importance and Shakespearean connections.

Horses can win over distances at Warwick that they would fail to get on rather more testing courses. In general, this track is appreciated by handy types that are able to cope with its sharp turns and by fast, front runners who relish its short run-in. It is ill-suited to horses that are one-paced or which need time to settle. Warwick also takes some riding, as jockeys who have failed to keep in touch in the early stages of sprints have found to their cost.

The course, 21 miles from Birmingham and 17 from Rugby, lies

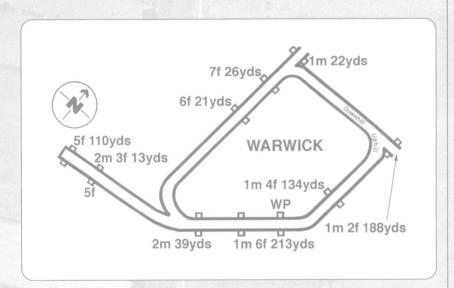

WARWICK: Plans of the Flat course (top), and the National Hunt course (bottom).

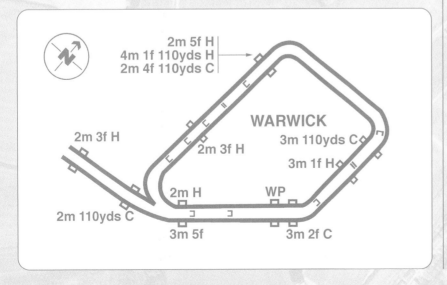

Warwick

close to the A46 Stratford to Coventry road (more accessible now the M40 joins this). It is less than three miles to the course by bus or taxi from Leamington station served by Paddington.

National Hunt racing is also staged at Warwick, most spectacularly via the Warwick National and the Crudwell Cup (which commemorates a prolific steeplechase winner of the 1950s). The former is the better-known contest and is often fiercely contested, while the latter is a handicap 'chase staged over 3 miles and almost 5 furlongs in early March. Warwick's most valuable jump race is the Warwickshire Gold Cup that is staged in early January.

Some fairly stiff fences (five of which have to be jumped in quick succession in the back stretch) make up the 'chasing circuit whose fairly sharp bends and occasionally undulating terrain can unsettle some jumpers. In general, adaptable, speedy National Hunt runners are favoured at Warwick, as are front runners since the run-in is short at 240 yards. Warwick has several boxes for hire at reasonable rates – just one of the enticing facilities provided by its progressive management.

Wetherby

This left-handed, oval-shaped jumping course is occasionally undulating; it features a rise to the winning post that continues after it has been passed and ground that descends into the long finishing straight with its short run-in of around 200 yards from the final obstacle.

The course is 12 furlongs in extent and is widely regarded as a testing one, thanks in part to the uphill finish and to its nine formidable fences which are, after those at Aintree on the Grand National circuit, regarded as the stiffest in Britain. There are five fences in the back stretch and four in the home straight. The first fence in the home straight and the second along the far straight are open ditches, while the water jump is in the middle of the five 'out in the country'.

Wetherby tends to be appreciated by fearless, bold-jumping, resolute, long-striding gallopers who can stretch out over its long straights. Such animals need to be able to cope with the track's two very abrupt and tight bends. The first of these is a very tight left-hander of 90 degrees or so that follows a long back straight on which the five obstacles are positioned so they can be readily viewed from the stands. The second last fence is particularly formidable.

The hurdle course here is a sharp, 10-furlong affair and a horse well rated on time often runs well on this if its jockey has a chance to put a foot down on the long straight.

Wetherby is popular with the racing fraternity partly because of the very fair, but searching, test it imposes on jumpers (which is why so many established and promising stars are sent here) and partly because it is so well appointed, comfortable and friendly. Another reason for the popularity of this picturesque course is the quality of its fixtures.

Perhaps the most widely known Wetherby steeplechase is the Rowland Meyrick Handicap Chase, an often thrilling contest staged at the popular Christmas meeting. Such well-seasoned performers as Cheltenham Gold Cup winners The Thinker and Forgive 'n Forget have prevailed in past runnings of this 3 mile 1 furlong 'chase.

Another prestigious 'chase is the Charlie Hall Chase, which is contested at the end of October. Past winners of this once again include Forgive 'n Forget, as well as Burrough Hill Lad and Wayward Lad (who won it twice).

Racegoers will find that Wetherby lies 12 miles north-east of Leeds, just south-east of the delightful Yorkshire

Wetherby Racecourse
York Road
Wetherby
West Yorkshire LS22 5EJ
Tel: (01937) 582035
www.wetherby.co.uk

HOW TO GET THERE:
From North: A1; B1224; A68 (from Thirsk); A1; B1224
From South: A1(M); A1; B1224
From East: B1224 (from York); A59
From West: A59 (from Harrogate); A661; B1224
By Rail: Harrogate; Leeds; York
By Air: Helicopter facilities

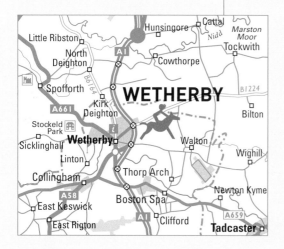

town of Harrogate, some nine miles away. The track benefits from its proximity to the Yorkshire training centre at Malton and also to the A1, which is the logical choice of route for those arriving from the north or south.

Motorists travelling from York should take the B1224. There is a rear exit from the course car park which gives access to the A1.

Rail travellers, many of whom leave from London King's Cross, will find that fairly long taxi-rides will need to be taken from either Leeds, York or Harrogate, while air travellers can be accommodated on-course if arriving by helicopter.

The course's excellent facilities allow spectators to view the paddock area without having to venture out into the cold. One of the charms of this course is that, since the grandstands are at an angle, spectators can enjoy virtually a head-on view of the last four fences.

Racegoers' facilities were further improved with the opening of the £4 million Millennium Stand in February 2000.

WETHERBY: Plan of the course.

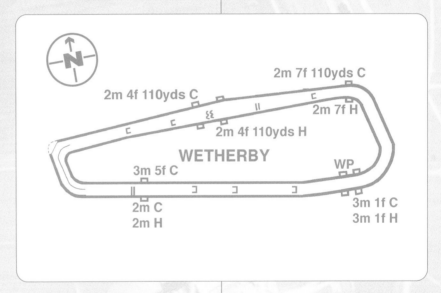

Wetherby

Wetherby

Wincanton

Wincanton Racecourse
Wincanton
Somerset BA9 8BJ
Tel: (01963) 32344
www.wincantonracecourse.co.uk

HOW TO GET THERE:
From North: M5 (Junct. 25); A358; A372; A303; B3081
From South: A352 (from Dorchester); B3145; B3081; A359 (from Yeovil); A303; B3081
From East: A303; B3081
From West: M5 (Junct. 25); A358; A372; A303; B3081
By Rail: Templecombe (four miles); Gillingham (six miles); courtesy bus to course
By Air: Airports at Bristol, Bournemouth, Exeter; Helicopter facilities

This right-handed racecourse, situated in the heart of the Somerset countryside, midway between the towns of Yeovil and Frome in a picturesque part of the West Country, is easily accessible both to Lambourn yards and many local handlers. Thus it continues to be popular and has frequently been voted the Best Small Racecourse in the South West by the Racegoers' Club. It is 11 furlongs round and rather like a cross between an oval and a quadrilateral. Its nine fences have been stiffened in recent years.

There is a short run-in of around 200 yards and spectators get an excellent view, particularly of the last three obstacles in the finishing straight. Given its two long straights, Wincanton is quite a galloping course that undulates mildly. There is rising ground once the winning post has been passed and a last turn downhill into the long finishing straight. Horses need to be able to race right-handed and also cope with the testing fences; front runners often poach leads that are unassailable on the short run-in from the last.

Rail travellers can reach the course from London Waterloo by travelling to Templecombe, Gillingham or Castle Cary, and then taking a taxi for a further seven miles. Once in the town of Wincanton, motorists should proceed northwards beyond it for a mile or so on the B3081.

Some of the major races staged on this east Somerset track are the Kingwell Hurdle and the 2 mile 5 furlong Desert Orchid Pattern Chase, run in October in honour of one of Britain's best-loved 'chasers. The Badger Brewery Chase has been run over 3 miles 1½ furlongs and the Hangover Handicap Chase has come later.

WINCANTON: Plan of the course.

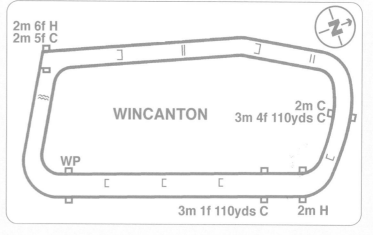

Windsor

Some races staged at Windsor have had names capitalizing on the course's proximity to a royal castle and its historic connections with England's foremost family. The most prestigious Windsor contest is the Winter Hill Stakes – a Group Three Event of 10 furlongs staged at a late-September fixture and three listed races, two of which take place at a two-day midsummer meeting.

Many Windsor races are twilight affairs, since about two-thirds of race meetings that take place here each season are staged in the evening. The majority of these are held on Monday nights; indeed 15 successive ones take place in May, June, July and August, Windsor's busiest months, during which minor miracles of restoration have to be carried out by the ground staff in order to maintain a good surface for racing.

Clearly the Windsor executive has great faith in evening racing since, not only does it provide more of this than any other British racecourse, but it does so just as soon (in the spring) and as long (until late in the summer) as is possible.

Windsor is very popular with both layers and their customers. Its often fine-sounding races tend to attract large fields of moderate sprinters and performers over 'intermediate' distances. This is because in 1966 the second right-handed loop was shortened and made over half as tight as it had been since its opening in Rays Meadows in 1865. Thus, after the former date, races could no longer be staged over 2½ miles 110 yards.

Windsor's short distances attract large fields of immature and non-staying animals. This is what makes racing here so competitive. It also explains why the course betting market has often been so strong. Some notable, even spectacular, 'coups' have been staged here.

The popularity of Windsor with the betting public can also be explained by its accessibility. In fact, it is one of the few racecourses that can be reached by air, land and water, since (by prior arrangement) helicopters can land here, trains run regularly from London Paddington and Waterloo to the nearby stations of either Windsor & Eton Central or Windsor & Eton Riverside, while a river bus from Windsor promenade takes racegoers to a racecourse jetty which is close to the paddock.

Moreover, the course is only 22 miles from central London. Those arriving via the M4 should leave at junction 6 and will find the track is just off the A308.

The racecourse itself is one of only two in Britain (the

The Racecourse
Maidenhead Road
Windsor
Berkshire SL4 5JJ
Tel: 0870 220 0024
www.windsor-racecourse.co.uk

HOW TO GET THERE:
From North: A25 (Junct. 15); M4 (Junct. 6, or 8/9); A355
From South: M23 (Junct. 8); M25 (Junct. 15); A308
From East: M20 (Junct. 3); M26; M25 (Junct. 15); A38
From West: M4 (Junct. 8/9)
By Rail: Windsor & Eton Riverside; Windsor & Eton Central
By Boat: River ferry
By Air: Helicopter facilities

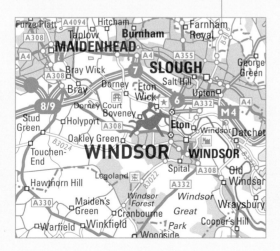

other is Fontwell) that describes a figure of eight. In doing so, it obviously features right- and left-hand bends. Interestingly, the latter are only negotiated by horses running in Windsor's longest races – those staged over 1 mile 3 furlongs 135 yards and 10 furlongs 7 yards.

Those tackling the former distance initially race over straight track that soon 'elbows' to the left. Next they encounter another straight stretch of track and then run round a slight and rather gradual left-hand bend that takes them into the longest straight section on the loop furthest from the stands. Those tackling 1 mile 67 yards at Windsor initially negotiate a spur that forms a short extension to its second loop.

On this the runners encounter a sharp, semi-circular, right-hand bend that runs into the sprint track, used for races over 5 furlongs 10 yards and 6 furlongs.

The ground hereafter continues to run the straight course it has followed since the longer sprint start until it 'elbows' to the right at the point where Windsor's two loops intersect, but not to such an extent that effectively foreshortens the run-in.

Thus, this can to all intents and purposes be regarded as a 5 furlong affair. Also, along with the track's many other shorter straight sections, it makes Windsor's frequent classification as a very sharp track rather inappropriate.

Jockeys have an opportunity to come with a long late run on long-striding, galloping types which are not as unsuited to Windsor as is popularly believed.

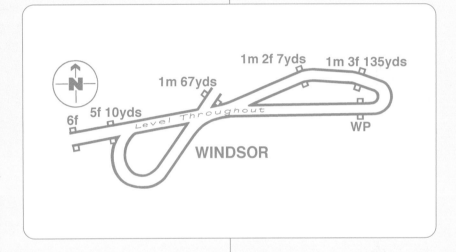

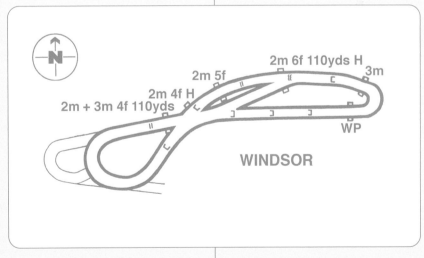

WINDSOR: Plans of the Flat course (top) and the National Hunt course (bottom).

Windsor

Windsor

Wolverhampton

Those who might formerly have been tempted to look down on Wolverhampton's once merely serviceable (but now 'state of the art') track ought to remember that in 1974 a horse that was beaten in a spring handicap restricted to apprentices and run over its largely flat and fair surface went on to win the Eclipse Stakes at Sandown Park!

This Midlands track, which offers a 'Brave New World' of racing is a purpose-built racecourse, complete with a pillar-free exhibitor hall. It is set in over 100 acres of Dunstall Park, a mile north-west of Wolverhampton's city centre and about the same distance from a railway station known as Wolverhampton High Level.

It is popular with both professional racing people and locals alike, and its regular Saturday evening meetings allow racing to be very comfortably savoured and combined with dancing until midnight! Local patrons and 'corporate' racegoers seem to appreciate the contrast it contributes to much of the industrial area in which it is located; it provided Britain's first Saturday evening fixture in July 1962. Intriguingly, one respondent to a survey of favoured love-making venues nominated the water jump once found at Wolverhampton's now defunct jumping track as his first choice!

While there is nothing really prestigious about most of the racing on this very fair course, it has a very distinctive flavour. This is because in time for Boxing Day 1993, Wolverhampton's previously pear-shaped track was transformed into an all-weather one. Thus was the dream fulfilled of Wolverhampton's supremo of 're-shaping horse racing entertainment' and the stage was set for regular Saturday evening racing, as well as for mid-week and Bank Holiday afternoon fixtures.

In August 1993, Tristram Ricketts, the then chief executive of the British Horseracing Board, described the new Wolverhampton complex as a 'very exciting development'. Thus the B.H.B. recognised that racing as a leisure business should offer its sporting service (via more than 60 race days at Wolverhampton) when people and betting shops need it and facilities that racegoers will find 'user-friendly'. At Wolverhampton there are brand new stadia, three restaurants that include a fully-glazed 400-seat facility, numerous private boxes and a racing museum, as well as a child care centre and adventure playground.

Thus the many millions spent on Wolverhampton's radical redevelopment has not only raised the profile of racing in the Midlands, but also brought the sport into the twenty-first century.

Wolverhampton Racecourse
Dunstall Park Centre
Gorsebrook Road
Wolverhampton WV6 0PE
Tel: (01902) 421421, 0870 220 2242
www.dunstallpark.co.uk

HOW TO GET THERE:
From North: M6 (Junct. 12); A5; A449
From South: M6 (Junct. 10A); M54 (Junct. 2); A449
From East: M6 (Junct. 10A); M54 (Junct. 2); A449
From West: M54 (Junct. 2); A449
By Rail: Wolverhampton High Level
By Air: Halfpenny Green Airport; Helicopter facilities

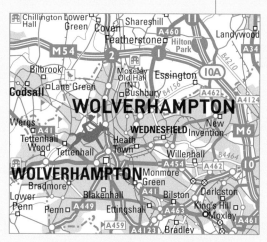

The all-weather circuit is a tight, left-handed affair that makes no great demands on jockeyship and provides racing surfaces that the ground staff take pains to preserve. Given its tightness, it suits sharp, short-striding types.

The course can be reached on the A449 from junction 12 of the M6, or from junction 2 of the M5. Wolverhampton's nearby railway station can be reached from Euston, while helicopters can land on-course if prior permission is obtained. Those arriving in fixed-wing aircraft need to make for Halfpenny Green, eight miles to the west of Wolverhampton.

Flat races run at Wolverhampton involve race distances of 2 miles 46 yards, 1 mile 6 furlongs 166 yards, 1 mile 4 furlongs, 1 mile 1 furlong 79 yards, 1 mile 100 yards, and 7, 6 and 5 furlongs, that are all staged on the all-weather course.

WOLVERHAMPTON: Plan of the all-weather Flat course.

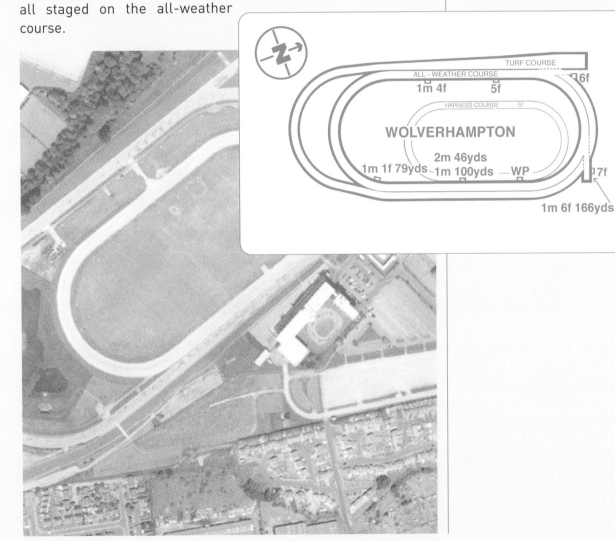

Worcester

Worcester's course, rated by authorities like Peter Scudamore as a fine steeplechasing circuit, is a flat, oval-shaped, left-hander of 13 furlongs which skirts the old flat-racing course.

There are easy, fairly sweeping turns and nine fences (five in the back stretch and four in the home straight) of a fairly average degree of difficulty, although some runners come to grief at the open ditch in the back straight. The finishing straight at Worcester, a long one of around 4 furlongs, contains four fences and ends in a 1-furlong run-in. Races over 2 miles 7 furlongs start in an extension to the far straight. All in all then, Worcester is a good galloping, very fair track that allows a novice to gain experience of jumping.

The track is close to the city centre and attractively situated in picturesque Pitchcroft Park (ideal for picnicking) next to the River Severn, which can make it waterlogged. However, when racing is frequently possible at Worcester, it proves highly popular with trainers from many parts of Britain. One measure of the course's popularity is the fact that it attracted a record entry for a National Hunt track – 229 runners on 13 January 1965.

Several races at a mid-August early-season fixture recall Edward Elgar's close association with Worcester; these include the Pomp and Circumstance Novices' Chase and the Enigma Handicap Hurdle.

The action has tended to hot up a little with the contesting of the Aga Novice Chase over 2 miles 7 furlongs in mid-November.

The course can be reached by rail via the nearby station of Worcester Foregate Street which lies on the London Paddington line.

The fact that Worcester is prone to waterlogging in wet winters perhaps explains why a wooden building in the course's central enclosure has served as the social club for local anglers lured by the River Severn. A race run at Worcester even recalls this prominent local feature.

Worcester Racecourse
Pitchcroft
Worcester WR1 3EJ
Tel: 0870 220 2772
www.worcester-racecourse.co.uk

HOW TO GET THERE:
From North: M5 (Junct. 6); A449
From South: M5 (Junct. 7); A38 (from Tewkesbury)
From East: A422 (from Alcester)
From West: A44 (from Leominster); A4103 (from Hereford)
By Rail: Worcester (Foregate Street)
By Air: Helicopter facilities

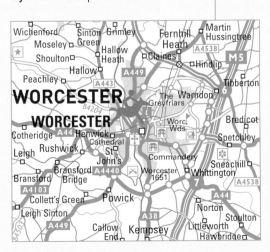

WORCESTER: Plan of the course.

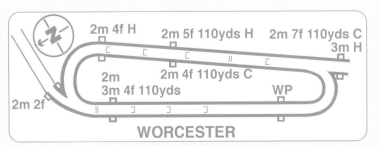

Worcester

Yarmouth

After Light Cavalry had triumphed in the 1980 St Leger, it emerged that his trainer, Henry Cecil, had given him a gallop on Yarmouth racecourse as part of his preparation for the final Classic.

The striking similarities between Yarmouth's 1¾ mile course (as it was then) and Doncaster's 14 furlong 132 yards were also appreciated and exploited by Joe Lawson who brought the 1954 Derby winner, Never Say Die, back to full fitness for the Doncaster Classic by running him at Yarmouth.

The Norfolk course is more of an oval than Doncaster and lacks the pear-like shape of this more prestigious course, but, far more crucially, both these largely flat tracks present long-distance performers with lengthy straights and a sharp final left-handed bend leading into a run-in of approximately 5 furlongs. It is often utilized by trainers as a course on which to test newcomers or progressive types.

Yarmouth's popularity with southern professionals is largely due to its proximity to Newmarket. Indeed, 18 out of the 19 races contested at a three-day meeting held here in September 1980 were won by horses from 'Headquarters' – many of them trained by some of the country's leading handlers; the horses that run at Yarmouth are often of far better class than those seen on other rather lowly racecourses. Many often run in rather humble maiden contests which, on their way to far better things, they generally win quite easily, if at fairly prohibitive odds.

There is a good deal about Yarmouth that explains why the races staged upon it are so extensively farmed by Newmarket handlers. It provides a surface for racing that can almost be guaranteed to be in good condition since it drains rapidly because there is so much sand in its subsoil. A run here imposes a far more revealing test than is obtainable on some rather easier racecourses, yet involves nothing that is harsh enough to sour an inexperienced runner.

The longest races staged on the round course, which extends for around 1½ miles, take place over 2 miles 2 furlongs 51 yards. They are started from the same point as events over 5 furlongs 43 yards. Stayers thus initially race over the entire length of Yarmouth's shortest sprint course.

Immediately after the winning post has been passed for the first time, long-distance performers at Yarmouth run round the first of the track's two semi-circular, tightish, left-

Yarmouth Racecourse
Jellicoe Road
Great Yarmouth NR30 4AU
Tel: (01493) 842527
www.greatyarmouth-
racecourse.co.uk

HOW TO GET THERE:
From North: M1; A1; A49; A149 (from Cromer)
From South: M11; A11; A47; A11 (from Lowestoft)
From West: A47 (from Norwich)
By Rail: Yarmouth Vauxhall
By Air: North Denes

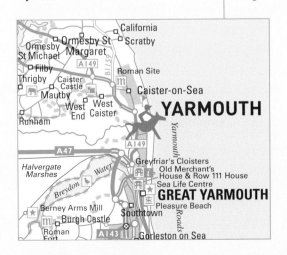

Yarmouth

YARMOUTH: Plan of the course.

hand bends. Next they pass the 11 furlong 101 yard start on the long back straight of 5 furlongs that runs almost parallel to the run-in.

After a final turn that is just as sharp as its predecessor, the round course joins the run-in that represents the last five-eighths of Yarmouth's straight 1 mile 3 yard course. This is a flat affair which apparently confers a slight advantage on the highly drawn if the stalls are positioned in the centre but, if they are placed on the far side, the lowly drawn enjoy a slight edge. The straight course is provided by a long spur which allows races over 1 mile 3 yards, 7 furlongs 3 yards, and 6 furlongs 3 yards to be staged. One of these, the Jack Leader Nursery Handicap, run over 7 furlongs 3 yards in mid-September, recalls a genial and well-known member of a famous Newmarket training family.

Since most of Yarmouth's meetings do not take place until

midsummer, its location on the coast is an added attraction. Londoners have only 126 miles to travel. There is one slight drawback about being a spectator at 'Newmarket-by-the-Sea': a raised section of the golf course within the oval track (once municipally owned and controlled) obscures one's view from the grandstand of some of the running on the back straight. However, this is a minor problem and no threat to the takings at the turnstiles.

One further reason why Yarmouth provides so much revenue is because, as a racecourse, it is so accessible. It lies on a bus route, is only a mile to the north of Yarmouth's town centre and its Vauxhall railway station can be reached fairly rapidly from Liverpool Street.

Motorists from London and the south should arrive via the M11, A11, and A47 via Norwich. Those coming from the north should progress beyond the M1 and A1 on the A47.

If racegoers are in a hurry they can always take a light aircraft or helicopter, and make, not for the course, but for North Denes airfield which is only about 300 yards away.

York

York Racecourse
York YO23 1EX
Tel: (01904) 620911
www.yorkracecourse.co.uk

HOW TO GET THERE:
From North: A1; A1(M) (Junct.
47); A59; A1237; A64; A19; A1036
From South: M1 (end); A64; A19
(from Selby)
From East: A166 (from Driffield);
A1079 (from Beverley)
From West: A59; A64
By Rail: York (1 mile)
By Air: Helicopter facilities

Although York is referred to by southerners as the 'Ascot of the North', most northern sportsmen and many professionals consider this a somewhat odious comparison, since, in some respects, York's three-day August festival is possibly a superior occasion.

Since market leaders tend to perform quite well at the main August meeting, it is popular with professionals, many of whom either take an early summer holiday during Ascot week or journey to the Berkshire course merely to join in the junketing and make notes on the running for future reference.

Despite its popularity with professionals, the Knavesmire is not a place where form always works out particularly well. Indeed, over the years some short-priced favourites have been sensationally beaten.

One particularly well-documented form upset was the defeat in 1851 of Voltigeur (the previous season's Derby and St Leger winner) by Flying Dutchman, a colt that had triumphed in these two particular Classics in 1849; an event witnessed by 100,000, mainly local, spectators.

In calling an 11 furlong 195 yard St Leger trial that is one of the highlights of the main August festival the 'Great Voltigeur Stakes', the York executive has thus acted more appropriately – especially since this particular colt also twice won the season's final Classic.

Naturally, many other top-class contests are staged on what is reputedly Lester Piggott's favourite British racecourse. Of several other Group races staged here, one, a highly regarded rehearsal for the Epsom Oaks, is the Musidora Stakes for three-year-old fillies, which is run over 10 furlongs 85 yards at the May meeting. This commemorates one of the late Captain Charles Elsey's very best horses, the filly that captured both the 1000 Guineas and the Oaks in 1949.

Also run over the same distance in mid-May is the Dante Stakes, an important Derby trial.

Another well-known race run at the May meeting (when the late-maturing grass on the Knavesmire is not always at its best) is the Yorkshire Cup over 13 furlongs 194 yards, a high-class event confined to horses of at least four years of age.

Apart from the Great Voltigeur Stakes, several other important races are staged at the August meeting. The most valuable of these is the International Stakes for three-year-olds and upwards which in its time, apart from

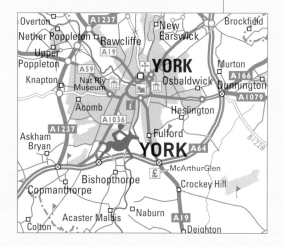

featuring some dramatic upsets, has been won by Derby winners Roberto and Troy, 2000 Guineas winners Wollow and Rodrigo de Triano, and St Leger hero Commanche Run.

The Yorkshire Oaks, like the International, has caused the undoing of several previously undefeated horses or acknowledged champions. In fact, several Epsom heroines have failed to prevail on the Knavesmire, possibly because by mid-August they had begun to 'train off'.

Noteworthy, too, on the festival programme are several races for two-year-olds. One of the most prestigious is the Lowther Stakes, a Group Two 6-furlong affair for two-year-old fillies.

The Gimcrack Stakes is another race for first-season performers staged over 6 furlongs during the August fixture. This contest commemorates a famous grey that won 26 of his 36 races. Although in recent seasons it has lost some of its kudos, the Gimcrack still attracts some of the best two-year-olds in training and on occasion is won by a horse that goes on to capture a Classic in its second season.

YORK: Plan of the course.

The Ebor Handicap, when it was first run over 1¾ miles in the middle of the nineteenth century, established a precedent at York, since races there had previously been staged over a gruelling 4 miles.

It is usually the chief betting race of the three-day August meeting, the highlight of its second day and a reminder of York's history since Ebor is a shortened version of Eboracum, the name the Romans gave to York (archaeological research suggests that they also held race meetings in this city).

Rather sadly, the 'Ebor' is now only listed as 'important'. However, it is still a competitive and rather spectacular contest. On the rare occasion when it is won by a runner with more than 8 st 7 lb on its back, then one can be sure that victory has gone to a really good horse. This was the case when Sea Pigeon, at the age of nine, triumphed in the 1979 running under the welter-weight of 10 st. Four-year-olds often go well in this stayers' handicap.

Meetings are also held at York in June and July and early in

September and October, and these all feature good-class sport. Many feature a famous race. One of these is the John Smith Magnet Cup, run over the International Stakes distance and the highlight of a Saturday card in July.

The York course takes some getting; indeed its negotiation involves a fairly gruelling test of stamina, especially if there is some give in the ground. It is for resolute, courageous types who relish a struggle.

As its very name of 'Knavesmire' suggests, York is not one of the fastest-draining racecourses, especially since its subsoil contains sufficient clay to make sticky going something of a certainty if it has rained fairly heavily prior to, or even during, a race meeting. By way of compensation, the moisture-retaining turf is seldom made hard by the heat of an average British summer.

While the track is sometimes likened to the letter 'U' or described as 'horseshoe-shaped', it is perhaps rather more reminiscent of a fish hook. It is wide and extends for 2 miles and, in general, it tends to suit long-striding, galloping types who can stretch out well and come with a late run on its extensive, near 5-furlong run-in.

Those taking part in 15 furlong 195 yard contests initially race along the far straight that extends for over ¾ mile alongside the Tadcaster road. Then, having passed the points from which races of 13 furlongs 194 yards, 11 furlongs 195 yards, and 10 furlongs 85 yards are started, they begin to sweep round the more gradual of York's two well-banked left-handed bends. Then, after passing the 1 mile 205 yard starting point, they continue to race along the shorter back straight, passing the 7 furlong 202 yard start and Knavesmire woods as they do so. Next they round York's second and rather sharper turn into its long finishing straight.

York's separate sprint course, which is initially provided by a spur of just over a furlong, allows races to be staged over 6 furlongs and the minimum distance. It is perfectly straight and tends to confer an advantage on the lowly drawn when the stalls are placed on the stands side or in the centre of the track.

The runners in 6 furlong 214 yard races initially negotiate a longish, tangential spur of 2 furlongs which runs into the middle of the final, almost semi-circular, but not excessively tight, final left-hand turn on the round course. This effectively means that this track forms something of a dog leg that is completed by York's long run-in of approximately 4½ furlongs.

As is to be expected of a course on which races are so often run at a fast pace, York takes some riding. Indeed, many shrewd judges have attributed Roberto's shock and fast time defeat of Brigadier Gerard in the 1972 running of the Benson and Hedges Gold Cup (now the International Stakes) in large part to his jockey Braulio Baeza, whose superb artistry and judgement of pace had already gained him a reputation.

It is also often to a jockey's advantage if he can place his mount in a handy position rounding the final turn.

The facilities at York match the splendour of the races. No wonder then that this impressive course often achieves the highest daily average attendance in the country. It also attracts the highest daily level of support from sponsors.

As for York's superb amenities, these are perhaps unrivalled on any British racecourse. A museum devoted exclusively to the sport of kings is housed in the grandstand, from which the racegoer can obtain such an excellent view of the proceedings. So attractive and luxuriously appointed are York's facilities that many of them are hired for varying functions on non-race days.

The layout of the public area also betokens much careful forethought by a commendable and open-handed executive. For example, terraces overlook the parade ring. In many ways the social calendar for August would never be quite the same were York races ever to disappear from it.

Racegoers should note that since the Knavesmire is virtually flat it can be taken at great speed. Thus, if one-paced animals take on top-class performers here, their limitations are likely to be ruthlessly exposed. Indeed, York is a track that tends to unsettle horses that cannot go the pace with powerful galloping types that like to make the running.

York is readily accessible. The city's railway station is not much more than a mile from the course and can be reached from London King's Cross. The A1 is an obvious and direct, if congested, route that brings many racegoers close to the city on race days.

Those travelling from further northwards should try to arrive via the A19. The considerate York management have previously arranged for light aircraft to land at Rufforth Aerodrome, some four miles west of York. In these circumstances, a landing fee is charged and transport can be arranged to the Knavesmire.

Index